太极拳竞赛套路中英对照学练指导丛书
A Chi...
Practi...

42式

竞赛套路

THE COMPETITION ROUTINE
OF 42 STYLE
TAI JI QUAN

主　编／张 山　Chief Editor / Zhang Shan

执行主编／武 冬　Executive Editor / Wu Dong

英文主编／李 伟　Editor of English Version / Li Wei

山西科学技术出版社

图书在版编目(CIP)数据

42 式太极拳竞赛套路/张山等主编.—太原:山西科学技术出版社,2003.3

(太极拳竞赛套路中英对照学练指导丛书)

ISBN 7 – 5377 – 2086 – X

Ⅰ.4… Ⅱ.张… Ⅲ.太极拳,四十二式—运动竞赛—套路(武术)—汉、英 Ⅳ.G852.111.9

中国版本图书馆 CIP 数据核字(2002)第 089084 号

---

42 式太极拳竞赛套路

作　　者:主　　编:张　山
　　　　　执行主编:武　冬
　　　　　英文主编:李　伟
出版发行:山西科学技术出版社
社　　址:太原市建设南路 15 号
邮　　编:030012
编辑部电话:0351 – 4922135
发行部电话:0351 – 4922121
E – mail:sxkjcbs@public.ty.sx.cn
　　　　　　Info@sxstph.com.cn
网　　址:http://www.sxstph.com.cn
印　　刷:山西新华印业有限公司人民印刷分公司
开　　本:850×1168　1/32
字　　数:128 千字
印　　张:5.5
版　　次:2003 年 3 月第一版
印　　次:2003 年 3 月第一次印刷
印　　数:1—5000 册
书　　号:ISBN 7 – 5377 – 2086 – X/Z·397
定　　价:16.80 元

前　言

　　太极拳是一项让世界人民着迷的具有丰富内涵的运动。自从面世以来，就以其独特的运动形式、深邃的文化底蕴、显著的健身效果吸引着越来越多的人们，特别是21世纪的到来，在高度文明、现代化的生活中，人们渴望自然、和谐的生活，健康、结实的体魄，太极拳恰好就是实现这些愿望绝好的运动。也正是因为如此，太极拳以其特有的方式发展着，从邓小平题词"太极拳好"到天安门万人太极拳表演，从城市到乡村，从中国到世界各地，到处都可以看到众多的太极拳习练者。现在，没有人能精确地计算出世界上到底有多少人在习练太极拳，世界上到底有多少个太极拳组织。然而，太极拳已经发展到世界每一个角落，阔步天下，是人所共知的。可是，由于种种原因，众多太极拳习练者往往因为没有好的教材而哀叹，特别是对世界各地的太极拳爱好者来说更是如此。太极拳竞赛套路是由国家颁布的一个规范的系列竞赛套路，同时也是一套健身的好教材。目前已经在中国乃至世界范围内推广开来。为了更好地配合世界各地的太极拳爱好者学好练好竞赛套路，我们特推出一套完整的、中英文对照的学练太极拳竞赛套路的指导丛书，以满足广大太极拳爱好者的需求。该丛书从学练太极拳的角度出发，高度概括出了行之有效的学练程序和手段，以简洁明快的语言直指动作的核心，大量的图解照片让您能无师自通。不仅如此,我们还随书配带光盘,为您提供动态的学练环境。书和光盘中的动作示范者均为有相当水准的太极拳教练。这您一看便知,我们的目的只有一个,就是献给广大读者一个精品。

尽管我们很努力,书中仍难免有错误之处,恳请广大读者多多指正!

愿太极拳带给您一生的快乐和健康!

愿我们的这套书对您能有所帮助!

编　者

Preface

Tai Ji Quan, which captivates the people all over the world, is a sports with rich connotations. Ever since it is introduced to the world, it attracts more and more people with the unique forms, the profound cultural characteristics and the remarkable affection on people's health. In the high civilized and modern 21 century, people seek for a more natural and harmonious life and a strong and healthy physique which are the function and purpose of Tai Ji Quan. And just because of these, Tai Ji Quan is developing fast on its own way from Deng Xiao – ping's inscription "Tai Ji Quan is good" to the demonstration done by 10 000 people in Tian An Men Square, from the cities to the countries and from China to the other countries in the world. Nobody can tell exactly how many people are learning and practicing Tai Ji Quan and how many organizations of Jai Ji Quan there are in the world. Unfortunately, the participants feel sorry and disappointed for not having a good and practicable book for them to follow, especially for those foreigners who know little about Chinese and Chinese Wu Shu. The competition routine of Tai Ji Quan is issued and

standardized by the nation for the purpose of the competition and keeping fit which becomes quite popular both in
China and in the world. In order to help the participants all
over the world for learning and practicing this routine, we
present this series of guide which is a Chinese – English
bilingual edition to meet your needs. This series illustrate
the easy and effective ways and procedures for learning
and practicing Tai Ji Quan and points out the key techniques of the movements with simple and lively words together with the tremendous photographs. In addition, we
also provide you the VCDs in which you can watch and follow the demonstrations done by the famous coaches. To
present you an excellency is the only purpose of this series.

Although we try hard to avoid mistakes, we may have
something that are not appropriate in this book and we sin-
cerely hope that you can help us to find out.

May Tai Ji Quan bring you happiness and health!

May this series meet your needs!

Editor

目 录

Contents

1.42 式太极拳竞赛套路简介

A Brief Introduction to the Competition Routine of 42 Style Tai Ji Quan

1.1　套路结构特点
The Characteristics in the Structure of the Routine

1.1.1　兼容性　Compatibility

42 式太极拳竞赛套路,是在广泛吸收了陈、杨、吴、孙、48 式等各式太极拳动作基础上,以杨式太极拳为主体创编而成的综合性竞赛套路,从套路编排到动作做法,都反映出了兼容各式太极拳的特点。

The competition routine of 42 style Tai Ji Quan was created based mainly on the Yang style while synthesizing the movements from several other Tai Ji Quan styles, such as Chen, Wu, Sun and the 48 styles. It is the comprehensive competition routine which reflects the characteristic of the compatibility of several different styles of Tai Ji Quan from the arrangement of the routine to the performance of the movements.

1.1.2　难度性　Considerable degree of difficulty

42 式太极拳竞赛套路,主要是为各级太极拳比赛而创编的,所以,在套路布局、动作数量、组别以及规格要求上具有相当的难度,特别是正式的武术锦标赛,还规定了指定动作,突出反映了 42 式太极拳套路的难度性。

The competition routine of 42 style Tai Ji Quan was mainly created for competing. So it is rather difficult in terms of its distri-

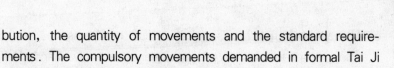

bution, the quantity of movements and the standard require-
ments. The compulsory movements demanded in formal Tai Ji
Quan championships most reflect the difficulty of 42 style Tai Ji
Quan.

1.1.3 差异性 Differentiability

42 式太极拳竞赛套路在动作编排上，吸收了各式太
极拳的动作，所以，尽管它最终统一于杨式太极拳的风格
特点，但是，还是有所差异。整个套路分为四段：

第一段以杨式太极拳动作为主体，外形舒展大方，柔
和缓慢。

第二段突出孙式开合手、吴式玉女穿梭、陈式掩手肱
捶的发力特点。

第三段以杨式云手、吴式打虎势等动作为主。突出
分脚、拍脚的高度控制和平衡，以锻炼稳定能力。

第四段基本上以 48 式太极拳的第四段为主，表现杨
式太极拳的风格特点。

Though the competition routine of 42 style Tai Ji Quan com-
plies with the characteristics of Yang style Tai Ji Quan, the arrangement of movements which absorbed from other Tai Ji Quan
is quite different. The whole routine can be divided into four seg-
ments:

Segment 1 mainly uses the movements of Yang style Tai Ji
Quan with the extensive posture and the slow and gentle performance.

Segment 2 emphasizes the characters of "opening and closing
hands" of Sun style Tai Ji Quan, "jade girl working with shuttles"

of Wu style and "hide hands and strike fist" of Chen style.

Segment 3 focuses on the movements of "wave hands like clouds" of Yang style and "beating tiger" of Wu style to practice the control and balance of toes kicking and slapping foot.

Segment 4 is based on the fourth segment of 48 style Tai Ji Quan which displays the characteristics of Yang style.

1.2　技术风格特点
The Characteristics in the Technique of the Routine

42 式太极拳已经成为十分普及的一个运动项目,其主要技术风格特点为:动作外形兼收各式,严格规范;动作气势恢弘大度,融为一体;动作衔接转接柔顺,简洁连贯;动作劲力以柔为主,兼有刚发;动作速度快慢有变,连绵不断。练法循规蹈矩,统一明确。

The 42 style Tai Ji Quan is very popular now. Its main technical characteristics are as the followings: The movements are stemmed from all other Tai Ji Quan styles and are standardized; the momentum of the movements is broad and well coordinated; the connection is smooth and coherent; the force is generated by the soft one and at times with the hard force; the speed of the movements has the changes of fast and slow. When practicing, perform the movements accurately and follow the clear demands.

2.42 式太极拳竞赛套路核心技术学练

Learning and Practicing the Key Techniques of the Competition Routine of 42 Style Tai Ji Quan

2.1 太极拳桩功练习
The Exercises of Tai Ji Quan Zhuang Gong

2.1.1 静桩 The motionless Zhuang Gong

桩功练习可以增强腿部静力性力量,提高对太极拳基本技术的认识,调息练意,不可轻视。

The main purpose of doing the motionless Zhuang Gong is to improve the potential leg strength, to prepare the body for basic Tai Ji Quan techniques and to enhance your breathing and awareness. Don't neglect this exercise.

图 2－1　Fig.2－1　　　　　图 2－2　Fig.2－2

2.1.1.1　浑圆桩(见图 2－1)。Primal position in chaos (Fig.2－1).

要点:两掌心斜相对丹田,中正安舒,深呼吸。

Key points: Make the two palms face "Dan Tian" and stand with your body relaxed and centered. Breathe deeply.

2.1.1.2　独立桩　分脚或蹬脚(见图 2－2～2－4)。
One leg stake　Toes kick or heel kick (Fig. 2－2～2－4).

要点:支撑稳定,身体中正。

Key points: Support your body steadily and keep it straight and centered.

图 2－3　Fig. 2－3　　　　　图 2－4　Fig. 2－4

2.1.2　动桩 The moving Zhuang Gong

2.1.2.1　进步(见图 2－5～2－12)。Advancing step (Fig. 2－5～2－12).

要点:重点是连续弓步之间的转换技术,由右弓步开始,左腿膝关节微屈,重心随之微后移,右胯根里抽,脚尖微翘,以右脚跟为轴,右腿在腰身的带动下,整体转动。右脚尖外摆45度左右,重心向右脚底下沉,左脚略蹬地辗转,松左胯根,左大腿带动左小腿,左脚通过身体的松沉,节节带动左腿,经过右脚内侧弧形上步,脚跟着地,松踝关节、膝关节,屈膝弓腿。同时,右腿蹬地劲力由脚而膝而腰胯,传于左腿,形成弓步,全身继续松沉,调整呼吸。此动作可以循环反复练习。

Key points: Focus on the changing techniques of the successive bow stance. Beginning with the right bow stance, bend your left leg and shift the weight gradually backward. Draw the right hip in and raise the right toes slightly. Turn the right leg by your waist using the right heel as the axis. Move the right toes out about 45 degree with the weight sunk on the right foot. Push the left foot against the ground and turn with the left hip relaxed. Use your left thigh to steer the movements of the left calf and foot. Relax your body and advance the left leg passing the inner side of the right foot and place the left heel on the floor. Relax the left ankle and bend the knee while pushing the right foot against the floor with the force transmitted from the right foot to the knee and then to the waist and hips to reach the left leg forming the bow stance. Continue to relax the whole body and adjust your breathing. This movement can be practiced repeatedly.

2.1.2.2　侧行(见图 2 – 13 ~ 2 – 16)。Side step (Fig.2 – 13 ~ 2 – 16).

要点:左脚横开一步,脚前掌先落地,依次放松膝踝关节,全脚掌落实,松左髋,重心左移,用腰带动右侧腿向左脚提收,保持身体重心的平稳移动。

Key points: Step the left foot aside with the ball of foot touching the floor and relax the knee and the ankle in turn. Drop the whole foot on the floor, relax the left hip and shift the weight to the left. Use your waist to steer the movements of raising and drawing the right leg inward and keep the weight of body moving steadily.

图 2 – 5 Fig.2 – 5

图 2 – 6 Fig.2 – 6

图 2 – 7 Fig.2 – 7

图 2 – 8 Fig.2 – 8

图 2 – 9   Fig. 2 – 9

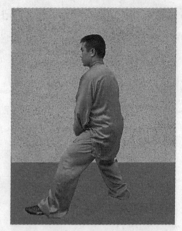

图 2 – 10   Fig. 2 – 10

图 2 – 11   Fig. 2 – 11

图 2 – 12   Fig. 2 – 12

图 2 - 13　Fig. 2 - 13

图 2 - 14　Fig. 2 - 14

图 2 - 15　Fig. 2 - 15

图 2 - 16　Fig. 2 - 16

2.2　核心技术动作练习
The Exercises of the Key Technical Movements

2.2.1　**搂膝拗步（见图** 2 – 17 ~ 2 – 23**）**。Brush knee and twist step（Fig. 2 – 17 ~ 2 – 23）.

图 2 – 17　Fig. 2 – 17　　　　　图 2 – 18　Fig. 2 – 18

　　要点：下肢要点同进步，上肢搂手与出腿、弓腿与推掌要配合，关键是后脚及全身的劲力要贯穿到推掌的手上。

　　Key points：The requirements for the lower limbs are similar to that of the advancing step. The brushing hand should be coordinated with the advancing leg and the bow stance should be coordinated with the pushing palm. The key is that the force generated from the back foot and the whole body should be penetrated into the pushing palm.

图 2 - 19　Fig.2 - 19

图 2 - 20　Fig.2 - 20

图 2 - 21　Fig.2 - 21

图 2 - 22　Fig.2 - 22

2.2.2　云手(见图 2 - 24 ~ 2 - 31)。Wave hands like clouds(Fig.2 - 24 ~ 2 - 31).

要点：下肢同侧行，手与脚都要在腰的带动下运动。

Key points: The require-ments for the lower limbs are similar to that of the side step. Use the waist to steer the move-ments of your hands and feet.

图 2 – 23　Fig. 2 – 23

图 2 – 24　Fig. 2 – 24

图 2 – 25　Fig. 2 – 25

图 2 – 26　Fig.2 – 26

图 2 – 27　Fig.2 – 27

图 2 – 28　Fig.2 – 28

图 2 – 29　Fig.2 – 29

图 2 – 30   Fig. 2 – 30   图 2 – 31   Fig. 2 – 31

3.42 式太极拳竞赛套路动作图解及要点

Photographs and Key Points of the Movements of the Competition Routine of 42 Style Tai Ji Quan

第一段 Segment 1

3.1 起势
Qi Shi (Commencing form)

3.1.1 并步站立(见图 3 - 1)。Stand with feet together(Fig. 3 - 1).

要点:思想集中在练拳上,用意识引导全身,从头到脚依次放松。做到心静用意,身正体松,虚领顶劲,气沉丹田,沉肩坠肘,含胸拔背,松腰敛臀,裆部圆虚,呼吸自然。

Key points: Concentrate on the movements and let your whole body relax from head to toes. Make yourself calm to straighten and relax your body. Relax your neck, keep your head aligned vertically with your body and inhale deeply into the abdomen. Drop your shoulders while keeping the elbows naturally down. Ease the chest inward while extending the back. Relax the waist with the buttocks

图 3 - 1　Fig. 3 - 1

tucked in. Keep the inner hip relaxed and breath naturally.

3.1.2 **左脚开立**(见图3-2~3-3)。Left foot steps aside(Fig. 3-2~3-3).

要点：左脚轻起轻落,开步身体重心平稳移动。请注意,起势的各项要求都要贯彻到以后的动作之中,万万不可忽视。

Key points：Raise and drop the left foot lightly. While opening the step, move your weight steadily across. Pay attention to the requirements of the commencing form, as they will be practiced throughout the routine. So do not neglect them.

图3-2 Fig.3-2   图3-3 Fig.3-3

3.1.3 **两臂平举**(见图3-4~3-5)。Raise arms forward and upward (Fig.3-4~3-5).

　　要点：全身向下松沉，劲起于脚，拔背沉肩，中指领劲，两臂自然平举，"一举动，周身俱要轻灵，尤需贯串"，"其根在脚"，最终形于手指。有个秘诀：想着走手不走肘，手臂自然升起。

图 3－4　Fig.3－4　　　　　图 3－5　Fig.3－5

Key points：Relax the whole body and the force is generated from the feet. Drop your shoulders, straighten the back and raise your arms forward naturally. "While raising the arms, the whole body should be agile and the feet are served as the roots." Make the force run to the fingers. In fact, the arms can rise up naturally when you move your hands instead of the elbows.

3.1.4　屈膝下按（见图 3－6）。Bend knees and press down (Fig.3－6).

　　要点：屈膝、按掌、两肘下沉，全身带动两掌下按，肘尖对地、坐腕，劲贯掌指。注意，坐腕不是成 90 度的死角，而是自然屈腕贯劲。这两个动作要连续不断劲，做到"无令丝毫间断耳"。哈哈，配合呼气下沉好舒服啊！

图 3 - 6 Fig. 3 - 6

Key points：Bend the knees, press the palms and drop the elbows. Use the body to steer the movement of pressing your palm downward with the palm facing forward and the fingers up and make the force reach the fingers. Remember to bend your wrist naturally and never form the angle at 90 degree. This two movements should be performed continuously without any breaking. You may feel very comfortable to exhale while dropping down.

3.2 右揽雀尾
You Lan Que Wei
（Right grasp the peacock's tail）

3.2.1 丁步抱球（见图 3 - 7 ~ 3 - 9）。T - stance and hold ball (Fig 3 - 7 ~ 3 - 9).

要点：身体向左侧松沉，用腰带动身体右转，劲贯右臂，两掌心相对。

Key points：Relax and drop the body to the left. Use your waist to turn your body right. The force is penetrated to the right arm with palm to palm.

图 3 - 7   Fig. 3 - 7   图 3 - 8   Fig. 3 - 8

图 3 - 9   Fig. 3 - 9

3.2.2   弓步左掤(见图 3 - 10 ~ 3 - 11)。Bow stance and Ward off (Fig. 3 - 10 ~ 3 - 11).

要点：左腿前弓由踝、膝、胯节节依次放松，与左臂协调一致，上下对应贯穿用劲，两臂撑圆。

图 3 - 10　Fig.3 - 10　　　　　图 3 - 11　Fig.3 - 11

Key points：Relax your ankle, your knee and your hips in turn to form the left bow stance and coordinate these movements with the left arm. The force runs through the legs and arms with the arms forming a circle.

3.2.3　丁步抱球（见图 3 - 12）。T - stance and hold ball（Fig.3 - 12）.

要点：左胯根收住，重心完全沉到左腿。然后，松右胯根，依次带动右腿收回成丁步，脚尖可以不落地，两掌合抱。

Key points：Draw the left hip in with the weight on the left leg . Relax the right hip to draw the right leg in to form T - stance.

Don't drop your toes to the floor and make the arms rounded.

图 3 – 12　　Fig.3 – 12

3.2.4 弓步右掤(见图 3 – 13 ~ 3 – 14)。Bow stance and Ward off (Fig.3 – 13 ~ 3 – 14).

要点:右脚上步时,左胯根抽住,膝关节不可前突过脚尖,或向里跪膝,右腿弓出、掤臂、松腰一致,动作完成时裆沉胯落,尾闾前收,脊背拔伸,气舒劲整。

Key points: While stepping the right leg foward, draw the left hip in and don't bend the right knee over the toes or inward. Coordinate the movements of making the right leg in bow stance, warding off with the left arm and relaxing the waist . When completing the movements, drop your groin and hips with "Wei Lu" drawn forward in, pull and straighten the back, breathe confortably and hold the force.

图 3 - 13 Fig.3 - 13   图 3 - 14 Fig.3 - 14

3.2.5 **后坐下将**(见图 3 - 15 ~ 3 - 18)。Sit back and deflect downward (Fig3 - 15 ~ 3 - 18).

要点：先松腰，前伸两掌。然后，重心后移，左胯根微开后撤，屈膝坐腿，松腰带动两掌侧将。

Key points：Relax your waist and stretch the palms forward. Move the weight backward and retreat the left hip slightly. Bend the knees and sit back. Relax your waist to steer the movement of palms deflecting to the side.

3.2.6 **弓步前挤**(见图 3 - 19 ~ 3 - 20)。Bow stance and squeeze forward (Fig.3 - 19 ~ 3 - 20).

要点：松右侧腰胯，身体调正，左脚蹬地，右腿前弓，松腰沉胯，挤手协调一致，劲贯右臂尺骨侧。

图 3 – 15　Fig.3 – 15　　　图 3 – 16　Fig.3 – 16

图 3 – 17　Fig.3 – 17　　　图 3 – 18　Fig.3 – 18

Key points: Relax your right hip and adjust your body straight and centered. Push the left leg against the floor and bend the right leg. Relax your waist and drop the hips while pressing hands forward. The force runs through the ulna of the right arm.

图 3 – 19   Fig.3 – 19   图 3 – 20   Fig.3 – 20

3.2.7 **后坐屈肘**(见图 3 – 21 ~ 3 – 23)。Sit back and bend elbow (Fig.3 – 21 ~ 3 – 23).

要点：松身坐腿带动右臂屈肘回收。

Key points：Relax your body and sit back on the hips to steer the movements of bending the right elbow and drawing it in.

3.2.8 **扣脚旋掌**(见图 3 – 24)。Turn foot inward and rotate palm (Fig.3 – 24).

要点：收右胯，扣脚左转身，以腰带动两臂平摆，右掌旋掌推出，上体端正。

Key points：Draw your right hip in. Turn the toes inward and the body left. Use your waist to steer the movement of swinging the arms. Rotate and push the right palm with your body straight.

图 3 – 21   Fig. 3 – 21

图 3 – 22   Fig. 3 – 22

图 3 – 23   Fig. 3 – 23

图 3 – 24   Fig. 3 – 24

3.3 左单鞭
Zuo Dan Bian（Left single whip）

3.3.1 **提脚勾手(见图** 3 – 25 ～ 3 – 26**)。**Raise leg and hook hand（Fig. 3 – 25 ～ 3 – 26）.

要点：重心移到右腿，虚实分清，提勾、提脚协调完成。

图 3 – 25　Fig. 3 – 25　　　　图 3 – 26　Fig. 3 – 26

Key points：Shift your weight to the right leg with distinct emptiness and solidness. Coordinate the movements of the lifting hook and the lifting leg.

3.3.2 弓步单鞭(见图3－27～3－28)。Bow stance and Single whip (Fig.3－27～3－28).

要点:左掌与弓左腿配合不先不后完成,左手、左脚尖、鼻尖,以及右手与右脚之间要对应相合。

Key points: Release the left palm and bend the left leg at the same time. Align the left palm, the left toes and the tip of nose and coordinate the movements of the right palm and the right foot.

图3－27 Fig.3－27   图3－28 Fig.3－28

3.4 提手
Ti Shou（Lift hands）

3.4.1 **扣脚摆掌**（见图 3 – 29）。Turn foot inward and sway palm（Fig.3 – 29）.

图 3 – 29 Fig.3 – 29

图 3 – 30 Fig.3 – 30

3.4.2 **回腰带掌**（见图 3 – 30）。Turn waist to steer palm（Fig.3 – 30）.

要点：松胯转腰来回带动两臂。

Key points：Relax the hips and turn the waist to steer the movement of the arms.

3.4.3 虚步合提(见图3－31)。Empty stance and close hands (Fig.3－31).

要点:含有上提之意。

Key points: Do this move with a sense of lifting up.

图 3－31　Fig.3－31　　　　图 3－32　Fig.3－32

3.5　白鹤亮翅
Bai He Liang Chi
（White crane spreads wings）

3.5.1 转身抱球(见图3－32～3－34)。Turn body and hold ball (Fig.3－32～3－34).

图 3 – 33   Fig.3 – 33

图 3 – 34   Fig.3 – 34

3.5.2   **转腰提掌(见图 3 – 35)。** Turn waist and raise palm (Fig. 3 – 35).

图 3 – 35   Fig.3 – 35

图 3 – 36   Fig.3 – 36

3.5.3　**虚步分手**(见图 3 – 36)。Empty stance and Separate hands (Fig. 3 – 36).

　　要点：两臂弧形撑开，在沉稳中有上拔的气势。

Key points: Open your arms in an arc form with a pulling force.

3.6　左右搂膝拗步
Zuo You Lou Xi Ao Bu
（Brush knee and twist steps on both sides）

3.6.1　**转体落手**(见图 3 – 37 ~ 3 – 38)。Turn body and drop hands (Fig. 3 – 37 ~ 3 – 38).

　　要点：两侧腰身依次放松带动两臂升降。

Key points: Relax both sides of the body in turn to steer the movements of moving arms up and down.

3.6.2　**收脚举掌**(见图 3 – 39 ~ 3 – 40)。Withdraw foot and lift arm (Fig. 3 – 39 ~ 3 – 40).

3.6.3　**迈步屈肘**(见图 3 – 41)。Step out forward and bend elbow (Fig. 3 – 41).

图 3 – 37　Fig.3 – 37

图 3 – 38　Fig.3 – 38

图 3 – 39　Fig.3 – 39

图 3 – 40　Fig.3 – 40

3.6.4　弓步搂推(见图 3 – 42 ~ 3 – 43)。Bow stance and brush push (Fig.3 – 42 ~ 3 – 43).

要点:两脚横向约 30 厘米。

Key points: The distance between your two feet is about 30 centimeters.

图 3－41 Fig.3－41   图 3－42 Fig.3－42

3.6.5 **转体摆脚**(见图 3－44)。Turn body and move foot outward (Fig.3－44).

要点:重心略后移,脚尖离开地面即可。

Key points: Shift your weight back slightly with the toes raised up from the floor.

3.6.6 **收脚举掌**(见图 3－45～3－46)。Withdraw foot and lift arm (Fig.3－45～3－46).

图 3 – 43   Fig.3 – 43

图 3 – 44   Fig.3 – 44

图 3 – 45   Fig.3 – 45

图 3 – 46   Fig.3 – 46

3.6.7   **迈步屈肘**(见图 3 – 47)。Step out forward and bend elbow (Fig.3 – 47).

3.6.8 弓步搂推(见图 3 – 48 ~ 3 – 49)。Bow stance and brush push (Fig. 3 – 48 ~ 3 – 49).

图 3 – 47　Fig. 3 – 47

图 3 – 48　Fig. 3 – 48

图 3 – 49　Fig. 3 – 49

要点:同左搂膝拗步。这里一共做了 2 次搂膝拗步,主要用到了连续的进步技术,可以再重温一下前边的核心技术练习。

Key points: Similar to "brush knee and twist steps" on both sides. The movement which is performed twice here employs the continuous advancing techniques. We can review the former key techniques while performing it.

3.7 撇身捶
Pie Shen Chui
(Dodge body and throw fist)

3.7.1 **转身分掌**(见图 3 - 50 ~ 3 - 51)。Turn body and separate palms (Fig. 3 - 50 ~ 3 - 51).

要点:重心略后移,不要完全坐在后腿。

Key points: Shift your weight back but don't totally sit on your hips.

3.7.2 **收脚落掌**(见图 3 - 52)。Withdraw foot and put down palm (Fig. 3 - 52).

图 3 – 50   Fig. 3 – 50

图 3 – 51   Fig. 3 – 51

1323 图 3 – 52   Fig. 3 – 52

3.7.3   上步翻拳(见图 3 – 53 ~ 3 – 54)。Step forward and turn fist over (Fig. 3 – 53 ~ 3 – 54).

3.7.4 弓步撇拳(见图 3 - 55)。Bow stance and block hand fist (Fig. 3 - 55).

图 3 - 53　Fig. 3 - 53　　　　　　图 3 - 54　Fig. 3 - 54

1326 图 3 - 55　Fig. 3 - 55

要点：用转腰以及手臂的合力贯到拳背。

Key points: Penetrate the force collected from turning your waist and arms to the back of the right fist.

3.8 捋挤势
Lu Ji Shi (Deflect and squeeze)

3.8.1 **扣脚变掌**(见图 3 - 56 ~ 3 - 57)。Turn foot inward and change palm (Fig.3 - 56 ~ 3 - 57).

图 3 - 56   Fig.3 - 56   图 3 - 57   Fig.3 - 57

3.8.2 **转体抹掌**(见图 3 - 58)。Turn body and feel palms (Fig.3 - 58).

图 3－58   Fig. 3－58   图 3－59   Fig. 3－59

3.8.3 收脚捋掌（见图 3－59）。Withdraw foot and deflect palm (Fig. 3－59).

要点：捋掌用腰身带动。

Key points：Use the waist to steer the movement of deflecting back with palms.

3.8.4 上步搭手（见图 3－60）。Step foward and place hand (Fig. 3－60).

3.8.5 弓步前挤（见图 3－61）。Bow stance and press forward (Fig. 3－61).

图 3 – 60   Fig. 3 – 60

图 3 – 61   Fig. 3 – 61

3.8.6 扣脚开掌(见图 3 – 62)。Turn foot inward and open palms (Fig. 3 – 62).

图 3 – 62   Fig. 3 – 62

3.8.7 **转体抹掌**(见图 3 – 63 ~ 3 – 64)。Turn body and feel palms (Fig.3 – 63 ~ 3 – 64).

图 3 – 63　Fig.3 – 63　　　　　图 3 – 64　Fig.3 – 64

3.8.8 **收脚将掌**(见图 3 – 65)。Withdraw foot and deflect palm (Fig.3 – 65).

3.8.9 **上步搭手**(见图 3 – 66)。Step forward and place hand against wrist (Fig.3 – 66).

3.8.10 **弓步前挤**(见图 3 – 67)。Bow stance and press forward (Fig.3 – 67).

图 3 – 65   Fig. 3 – 65   图 3 – 66   Fig. 3 – 66

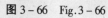

图 3 – 67   Fig. 3 – 67

3.9 进步搬拦捶
Jin Bu Ban Lan Chui
（Advance, parry and punch）

3.9.1 **摆脚分臂**（见图 3 – 68 ~ 3 – 69）。Turn foot outward and separate arms（Fig. 3 – 68 ~ 3 – 69）.

图 3 – 68 Fig. 3 – 68   图 3 – 69 Fig. 3 – 69

3.9.2 **收脚挂臂**（见图 3 – 70 ~ 3 – 71）。Withdraw foot and punch down（Fig. 3 – 70 ~ 3 – 71）.

3.9.3 **上步搬拳**（见图 3 – 72）。Step forward and punch（Fig. 3 – 72）.

图 3 – 70   Fig. 3 – 70

图 3 – 71   Fig. 3 – 71

要点：松腰胯,沉裆劲,迈步轻灵平稳。左掌下压与右拳搬出同时,幅度不宜超过胸的宽度。

Key points: Relax your waist and hips, drop your groin and step forward with the agility and steadiness. Press the left palm down while punching and don't exceed the width of the chest.

图 3 – 72   Fig. 3 – 72

3.9.4　**转身拦掌**(见图 3 – 73 ~ 3 – 74)。Turn body and parry palm (Fig.3 – 73 ~ 3 – 74).

图 3 – 73　Fig.3 – 73　　　　　　　　　图 3 – 74　Fig.3 – 74

3.9.5　**弓步打捶**(见图 3 – 75)。Bow stance and punch (Fig.3 – 75).

要点:拦掌、打拳与弓腿协调一致,弓步的两脚横向距离约为 10 厘米。

Key points: Coordinate the movements of bending leg, parrying and punching. The distance between your two feet is about 10 centimeters.

图 3 – 75　Fig. 3 – 75

3.10　如封似闭
Ru Feng Si Bi（Apparent close up）

3.10.1　穿手翻掌（见图 3 – 76 ~ 3 – 77）。Pierce hands and turning palms（Fig. 3 – 76 ~ 3 – 77）.

3.10.2　后坐收掌（见图 3 – 78）。Sit back and withdraw palms（Fig. 3 – 78）.

　　要点：松腰、沉胯，身体后坐带动两臂屈肘收掌，上体中正，下肢圆裆开胯。

　　Key points：Relax your waist and drop the hips. Sit back to

bend the elbows and draw the palms back. Keep the upper body straight and centered with the round groin and relax the hips.

图 3－76　Fig.3－76　　　　图 3－77　Fig.3－77

图 3－78　Fig.3－78　　　　图 3－79　Fig.3－79

3.10.2 翻掌落掌(见图 3 – 79)。Turn and drop palms (Fig. 3 – 79).

3.10.4 跟步推按(见图 3 – 80 ~ 3 – 81)。Follow up step and push press (Fig. 3 – 80 ~ 3 – 81).

要点：裆劲下沉，右脚蹬地，两掌随重心前移，浅弧形推出。

Key points: Drop your groin and push your right foot against the floor. Shift your weight while pushing the palms forward in an arc route.

图 3 – 80   Fig. 3 – 80   图 3 – 81   Fig. 3 – 81

第二段　Segment　2

3.11　开合手
Kai He Shou
（Open and close hands）

3.11.1　**转体开掌**(见图 3 – 82 ~ 3 – 83)。Turn body and open palms (Fig. 3 – 82 ~ 3 – 83).

　　要点:转体与开手,在转腰带动下,边转体边完成,开掌时两掌心始终相对,利用身体内部的运动,催动两掌分开,重心略右移。

图 3 – 82　Fig. 3 – 82　　　　　图 3 – 83　Fig. 3 – 83

Key points: Perform the movements of turning your body and opening the palms simultaneously by turning your waist. Use the movement of the chest to steer the movement of opening the palms with palms always facing each other and shift your weight to the right leg.

3.11.2　提踵合掌(见图 3 – 84 ~ 3 – 85)。Raise heel and close palms (Fig. 3 – 84 ~ 3 – 85).

要点：重心略左移,从外表上看不出明显的移动,呼气合掌,两掌之间相系相吸,含胸扩背。两肘尖始终下坠,肩部不可耸起。如果你做对了,会感到胸背胀展,两掌心有开中吸,合中开的气感。

图 3 – 84　Fig. 3 – 84　　　　图 3 – 85　Fig. 3 – 85

Key points: Shift your weight slightly to the left, and exhale and close your palms. Draw your chest in and expand the back with the palms facing each other. Drop the elbows and don't shrug the shoulders. If you do it correctly, you will feel the expanding of the chest and the back and the sensation of the "Qi" while performing.

3.12 右单鞭
You Dan Bian（Right single whip）

3.12.1 开步翻掌（见图 3 − 86）。Open step and turn palm（Fig. 3 − 86）.

图 3 − 86 Fig. 3 − 86   图 3 − 87 Fig. 3 − 87

3.12.2 横步单鞭（见图 3 − 87）。Step aside and single whip（Fig. 3 − 87）.

要点：下肢开胯、屈膝撑圆，两掌边向外推，左右横开。就像双手将一根长杆。

Key points：Open your hips and bend the knees. Push the palms outward and opened to either side just like stroking a long pole with two hands.

3.13 肘底捶
Zhou Di Chui（Fist under elbow）

3.13.1 **扣脚摆掌(见图**3－88～3－89**)。**Turn foot inward and sway palm（Fig.3－88～3－89）.

图3－88 Fig.3－88　　　　　图3－89 Fig.3－89

3.13.2 **收脚抱球**(见图 3 – 90 ~ 3 – 92)。Withdraw foot and hold ball (Fig. 3 – 90 ~ 3 – 92).

要点:左右倒换重心时不可身体明显起伏。

Key points: While shifting your weight left or right, don't raise the body up or down.

图 3 – 90　Fig. 3 – 90　　　　图 3 – 91　Fig. 3 – 91

3.13.3 **转体分掌**(见图 3 – 93 ~ 3 – 95)。Turn body and open palms (Fig. 3 – 93 ~ 3 – 95).

要点:以腰脊为轴带动两臂平抹。

Key points: Use the waist and the backbone as the axis to steer the movements of the arms.

图 3 – 92   Fig. 3 – 92

图 3 – 93   Fig. 3 – 93

3 – 94   Fig. 3 – 94

图 3 – 95   Fig. 3 – 95

3.13.4 跟步摆掌(见图 3－96)。Follow up step and sway palm (Fig.3－96).

图 3－96　Fig.3－96　　　　图 3－97　Fig.3－97

3.13.5 虚步藏拳(见图 3－97)。Cover fist and empty stance (Fig.3－97).

要点:重心虚实分清,四肢屈蓄有余。

Key points: Shift your weight with the distinct emptiness and the solidness. Bend the limbs to collect the force.

3.14 转身推掌
Zhuan Shen Tui Zhang
（Turn body and push palm）

3.14.1 **转体举掌**（见图 3 – 98 ~ 3 – 99）。Turn body and raise palms（Fig. 3 – 98 ~ 3 – 99）.

图 3 – 98   Fig. 3 – 98   图 3 – 99   Fig. 3 – 99

3.14.2 **转体屈肘**（见图 3 – 100）。Turn body and bend elbows （Fig. 3 – 100）.

要点：右脚微内扣再转体。
Key points：Turn the right foot inward and turn your body.

60

图 3 – 100　Fig.3 – 100　　　图 3 – 101　Fig.3 – 101

3.14.3　**跟步推掌(见图 3 – 101)。** Follow up step and push knee (Fig.3 – 101).

要点:转体时,左臂保持圆形。

Key points: While turning the body, keep the left arm rounded.

3.14.4　**转身举掌(见图 3 – 102 ~ 3 – 103)。** Turn body and raise palm (Fig.3 – 102 ~ 3 – 103).

3.14.5　**上步屈肘(见图 3 – 104)。** Step foward and bend elbow (Fig.3 – 104).

要点:左脚微内扣再转体。

Key points: Turn the left foot inward and turn your body.

图 3 – 102   Fig.3 – 102   图 3 – 103   Fig.3 – 103

图 3 – 104   Fig.3 – 104

3.14.6 跟步推掌(见图 3 – 105 ~ 3 – 106)。Follow up step and push palms (Fig.3 – 105 ~ 3 – 106).

图 3－105　Fig.3－105　　　　图 3－106　Fig.3－106

3.15　左右穿梭
Zuo You Chuan Suo
（Jade girl working with shuttles on both sides）

3.15.1　撤步伸掌(见图 3 - 107 ~ 3 - 108)。Retreat step and stretch palms (Fig.3 - 107 ~ 3 - 108).

3.15.2　收脚捋掌(见图 3 - 109 ~ 3 - 111)。Withdraw foot and deflect palm (Fig.3 - 109 - 3 - 111).

图 3 – 107   Fig.3 – 107

图 3 – 108   Fig.3 – 108

图 3 – 109   Fig.3 – 109

图 3 – 110   Fig.3 – 110

3.15.3   上步掤臂（见图 3 – 112）。Step forward and ward off arm（Fig.3 – 112）.

3.15.4 跟步摆掌（见图 3 – 113 ~ 3 – 114）。Follow up step and sway palm (Fig. 3 – 113 ~ 3 – 114).

图 3 – 111   Fig. 3 – 111

图 3 – 112   Fig. 3 – 112

图 3 – 113   Fig. 3 – 113

图 3 – 114   Fig. 3 – 114

3.15.5 上步旋掌(见图 3 – 115 ~ 3 – 117)。Step forward and rotate palm (Fig. 3 – 115 ~ 3 – 117).

图 3 – 115　Fig. 3 – 115　　　　图 3 – 116　Fig. 3 – 116

图 3 – 117　Fig. 3 – 117

3.15.6　**弓步架推**(见图 3 – 118 ~ 3 – 119)。Bow stance and block push (Fig.3 – 118 ~ 3 – 119).

　　要点:以身体垂直轴为轴,转腰带动手臂旋转,架掌肩不可上耸。

Key points: Turn your waist to steer the movement of twisting the arm by using the perpendicular of the body as the axis. Don't shrug the shoulders while blocking with the palms.

图 3 – 118　Fig.3 – 118　　　　图 3 – 119　Fig.3 – 119

3.15.7　**后坐落掌**(见图 3 – 120)。Sit back and drop palm (Fig.3 – 120).

3.15.8　**弓步抹掌**(见图 3 – 121)。Bow stance and feel palm (Fig.3 – 121).

图 3 – 120   Fig.3 – 120

图 3 – 121   Fig.3 – 121

图 3 – 122   Fig.3 – 122

图 3 – 123   Fig.3 – 123

3.15.9　收脚捋掌(见图 3 – 122)。Withdraw foot and deflect palm (Fig.3 – 122).

3.15.10 **上步掤臂**(见图 3 – 123)。 Step forward and ward off (Fig.3 – 123)．

3.15.11 **跟步摆掌**(见图 3 – 124 ~ 3 – 125)。 Follow up step and sway palm (Fig.3 – 124 ~ 3 – 125)．

图 3 – 124　Fig.3 – 124　　　　图 3 – 125　Fig.3 – 125

3.15.12 **上步旋掌**(见图 3 – 126)。 Step forward and rotate palm (Fig.3 – 126)．

3.15.13 **弓步架推**(见图 3 – 127)。 Bow stance and block push (Fig.3 – 127)．

图 3 – 126   Fig.3 – 126

图 3 – 127   Fig.3 – 127

3.16   右左蹬脚
You Zuo Deng Jiao
（Heel kick on both sides）

3.16.1   **后坐摆掌**（见图 3 – 128）。Sit back and sway palms （Fig.3 – 128）.

3.16.2   **转体分手**（见图 3 – 129 ~ 3 – 130）。Turn body and open palms （Fig.3 – 129 ~ 3 – 130）.

图 3 – 128   Fig.3 – 128

图 3 – 129   Fig.3 – 129

图 3 – 130   Fig.3 – 130

图 3 – 131   Fig.3 – 131

3.16.3   **收脚合手**(见图 3 – 131)。Withdraw foot and close palms (Fig.3 – 131).

要点：两掌相合要与提膝一致，右肘与右膝相对。

Key points：Closing palms should be coordinated with raising the knee. Align the right elbow and the right knee.

3.16.4 蹬脚分掌（见图 3 – 132）。Heel kick and open palms (Fig.3 – 132).

要点：分掌与蹬脚同时完成，手脚协调相合，头顶气沉，支撑腿不要僵直，膝微屈。

Key points：Open palms while kicking with the right heel. Keep your head up and the "Qi" down. Bend the supporting leg a little and don't stand stiff.

图 3 – 132　Fig.3 – 132　　　　图 3 – 133　Fig.3 – 133

3.16.5 落脚摆掌（见图 3 – 133）。Drop leg and sway palm (Fig.3 – 133).

3.16.6　**转体分掌**(见图 3 – 134 ~ 3 – 135)。Turn body and sep-arate palms (Fig. 3 – 134 ~ 3 – 135).

图 3 – 134　Fig. 3 – 134　　　　图 3 – 135　Fig. 3 – 135

3.16.7　**收脚合手**(见图 3 – 136)。Withdraw foot and close palms (Fig. 3 – 136).

3.16.8　**蹬脚分掌**(见图 3 – 137)。Heel Kick and separate palms (Fig. 3 – 137).

图 3 – 136   Fig. 3 – 136   图 3 – 137   Fig. 3 – 137

3.17   掩手肱捶
Yan Shuo Gong Chui
（Hide hands and strike fist）

3.17.1   **落脚掩掌(**见图 3 – 138 ~ 3 – 139**)。** Drop foot and cover palms（Fig. 3 – 138 ~ 3 – 139）.

3.17.2   **开步合掌(**见图 3 – 140**)。** Open step and close palms（Fig. 3 – 140）.

图 3－138　Fig.3－138

图 3－139　Fig.3－139

图 3－140　Fig.3－140

图 3－141　Fig.3－141

3.17.3　马步分掌（见图 3－141）。Horse stance and separate palms（Fig.3－141）.

3.17.4 转体合手(见图 3 – 142)。Turn body and close palms (Fig. 3 – 142).

图 3 – 142   Fig. 3 – 142

3.17.5 弓步冲捶(见图 3 – 143 ~ 3 – 144)。Bow stance and punch fist (Fig. 3 – 143 ~ 3 – 144).

要点:沉胯、转腰、腰脊发力,左手配合主动回抽。

Key points: Drop the hips and turn the waist. Release the force from the waist and the spine and pull back the left hand.

图 3 – 143   Fig.3 – 143   图 3 – 144   Fig.3 – 144

3.18   左右野马分鬃
Zuo You Ye Ma Fen Zong
（Parting the wild horse's mane on both sides）

3.18.1   转腰下捋（见图 3 – 145）。Turn waist and deflect（Fig.3 – 145）.

3.18.2   转腰捌臂（见图 3 – 146）。Turn waist and ward off（Fig.3 – 146）.

3.18.3 转腰横抖(见图 3 – 147 ~ 3 – 149)。Turn waist and shake (Fig.3 – 147 ~ 3 – 149).

图 3 – 145　Fig.3 – 145

图 3 – 146　Fig.3 – 146

图 3 – 147　Fig.3 – 147

图 3 – 148　Fig.3 – 148

3.18.4 回腰旋腕(见图 3 – 150 ~ 3 – 151)。Turn waist back and rotate wrist (Fig.3 – 150 ~ 3 – 151).

图 3 – 149　Fig.3 – 149

图 3 – 150　Fig.3 – 150

图 3 – 151　Fig.3 – 151

3.18.5 提膝托掌(见图 3 – 152 ~ 3 – 153)。Lift knee and raise palms (Fig. 3 – 152 ~ 3 – 153).

图 3 – 152　Fig. 3 – 152

图 3 – 153　Fig. 3 – 153

图 3 – 154　Fig. 3 – 154

图 3 – 155　Fig. 3 – 155

3.18.6　**弓步穿掌(**见图 3 – 154 ~ 3 – 155**)。** Bow stance and pierce palm (Fig.3 – 154 ~ 3 – 155).

3.18.7　**摆脚采按(**见图 3 – 156**)。** Turn foot outward and press palm (Fig.3 – 156).

图 3 – 156　Fig.3 – 156

3.18.8　**提膝托掌(**见图 3 – 157 ~ 3 – 158**)。** Lift knee and raise palm (Fig.3 – 157 ~ 3 – 158).

3.18.9 弓步穿掌（见图 3 – 159 ~ 3 – 160）。Bow stance and pierce palm（Fig.3 – 159 ~ 3 – 160）.

图 3 – 157　Fig.3 – 157

图 3 – 158　Fig.3 – 158

图 3 – 159　Fig.3 – 159

图 3 – 160　Fig.3 – 160

要点：此动作取材于陈式太极拳动作，重在用腰带动手臂。

Key points：This movement is taken from Chen style Tai Ji Quan which stresses on the movement of using the waist to steer the arms.

第三段　Segment　3

3.19　云手
Yun Shou（Wave hands like clouds）

3.19.1　**扣脚摆掌（见图3 – 161 ~ 3 – 162）。** Turn foot inward and sway palms（Fig.3 – 161 ~ 3 – 162）.

图3 – 161　Fig.3 – 161　　　图3 – 162　Fig.3 – 162

3.19.2 **转体翻掌(见图**3 – 163 ~ 3 – 164**)。**Turn body and palms（Fig.3 – 163 ~ 3 – 164）.

图 3 – 163　　Fig.3 – 163

图 3 – 164　　Fig.3 – 164

图 3 – 165　　Fig.3 – 165

图 3 – 166　　Fig.3 – 166

3.19.3 **转体云手**(见图 3 – 165 ~ 3 – 166)。Turn body and wave hands (Fig.3 – 165 ~ 3 – 166).

3.19.4 **收脚撑掌**(见图 3 – 167)。Withdraw foot and stretch palms (Fig.3 – 167).

要点:身体转动要以腰脊为轴,松腰、松胯,身体重心平稳移动,以腰贯穿手脚,上下协调运动。

Key points: Turn the body by using the waist as the axis. Relax the waist and hips, shift the weight across steady and use the waist to coordinate the movements of arms and legs.

图 3 – 167　Fig.3 – 167　　　　　图 3 – 168　Fig.3 – 168

3.19.5 **转体云手**(见图 3 – 168)。Turn body and wave hands (Fig.3 – 168).

3.19.6 **开步云手**(见图 3 – 169)。Open step and wave hands (Fig.3 – 169).

图 3 – 169　Fig.3 – 169　　　　图 3 – 170　Fig.3 – 170

3.19.7 **转体云手**(见图 3 – 170 ~ 3 – 171)。Turn body and wave hands (Fig.3 – 170 ~ 3 – 171).

图 3 – 171　Fig.3 – 171　　　　图 3 – 172　Fig.3 – 172

3.19.8　**收脚撑掌**（见图 3 – 172）。Withdraw foot and stretch palms (Fig.3 – 172).

　　要点：移动过程中腰略走后弧。

　　Key points：Move the waist backward in an arc route.

3.19.9　**转体云掌**（见图 3 – 173 ~ 3 – 178）。Turn body and wave palms (Fig.3 – 173 ~ 3 – 178).

图 3 – 173   Fig. 3 – 173

图 3 – 174   Fig. 3 – 174

图 3 – 175   Fig. 3 – 175

图 3 – 176   Fig. 3 – 176

图 3 – 177   Fig.3 – 177   图 3 – 178   Fig.3 – 178

3.20 独立打虎
Du Li Da Hu（Beat tiger on single leg）

3.20.1 撤步穿掌（见图 3 – 179 ~ 3 – 180）。Retreat step and pierce palms（Fig.3 – 179 ~ 3 – 180）.

3.20.2 转体扣脚（见图 3 – 181）。Turn body and turn foot inward（Fig.3 – 181）.

图 3 - 179   Fig.3 - 179   图 3 - 180   Fig.3 - 180

图 3 - 181   Fig.3 - 181

3.20.3　提膝抱拳(见图 3 - 182 ~ 3 - 183)。Lift knee and hold
fists (Fig.3 - 182 ~ 3 - 183).

要点：右肘对右膝。

Key points：Align the right elbow and the right knee.

图 3 - 182　Fig. 3 - 182　　　　图 3 - 183　Fig. 3 - 183

3.21　右分脚
You Fen Jiao（Right toes kick）

3.21.1　**提膝合手**（见图 3 - 184）。Lift knee and close palms
(Fig. 3 - 184).

要点：右脚不落地，左腿微屈。

Key points：Don't drop the right leg to the floor while the left
leg bended slightly.

图 3 – 184 Fig.3 – 184   图 3 – 185 Fig.3 – 185

3.21.2 **分脚撑掌**(见图 3 – 185)。Toes kick and stretch palm (Fig.3 – 185).

要点:分脚时脚尖不可过分用力,防止紧张发抖。

Key points: While separating the legs, do not tense the toes in case the leg will tremble.

3.22 双峰贯耳

Shuang Feng Guan Er

(Striking the opponent's ears with both fists)

3.22.1 **勾脚落手**(见图 3 – 186)。Hook feet and drop hand (Fig.3 – 186).

要点：右腿回屈时，意想勾挂。

图 3 - 186　Fig.3 - 186　　　　图 3 - 187　Fig.3 - 187

Key points: Bend the right leg back as if you were hanging it on a hook.

3.22.2 **上步落掌(见图 3 - 187)。** Step forward and drop palm (Fig.3 - 187).

3.22.3 **弓步双贯(见图 3 - 188)。** Bow stance and strike punch (Fig.3 - 188).

要点：两掌下落时利用松身沉胯的整劲，贯击时用扩背之劲贯于两拳眼。

Key points: Low down your palms by using the force collected from relaxing your body and hips. Move the force collected from expanding the back to the fist eyes and punch.

图 3 – 188　　Fig. 3 – 188

3.23　左分脚
Zuo Fen Jiao（Left toes kick）

3.23.1　**转体分掌**（见图 3 – 189 ~ 3 – 190）。Turn body and open palms（Fig. 3 – 189 ~ 3 – 190）.

3.23.2　**收脚合抱**（见图 3 – 191）。Withdraw foot and cross arms（Fig. 3 – 191）.

3.23.3　分掌分脚(见图 3 – 192)。Open palms and leg (Fig.3 – 192).

图 3 – 189　Fig.3 – 189

图 3 – 190　Fig.3 – 190

图 3 – 191　Fig.3 – 191

图 3 – 192　Fig.3 – 192

3.24 转身拍脚
Zhuan Shen Pai Jiao (Turn body and slap foot)

3.24.1 **落脚转身(**见图 3 – 193 ~ 3 – 194**)。** Drop foot and turn body (Fig.3 – 193 ~ 3 – 194).

图 3 – 193   Fig.3 – 193   图 3 – 194   Fig.3 – 194

3.24.2 **转体合手(**见图 3 – 195**)。** Turn body and close hands (Fig.3 – 195).

要点：转身时，先松右胯下沉，然后左腿松落，转腰带动身体转动，右脚跟不可高抬。

Key points：When turning your body, relax the right hip and

96

drop the left leg. Use the waist to steer the movement of turning the body and don't raise the right heel.

图 3 – 195   Fig. 3 – 195

3.24.3   **独立拍脚(见图** 3 – 196 ~ 3 – 197**)。**Slap foot on one leg (Fig. 3 – 196 ~ 3 – 197).

　　要点:用腰带动右腿的大腿、小腿以及脚与右手迎击拍响。右掌松拍脚面。

Key points: Use your waist to steer the movement of raising the right leg to meet the right hand. Relax the right palm to slap the right instep.

图 3 – 196　Fig.3 – 196　　　　图 3 – 197　Fig.3 – 197

3.25　进步栽捶
Jin Bu Zai Chui
（**Advance and punch down**）

3.25.1　**转体摆掌**(见图 3 – 198 ~ 3 – 199)。Turn body and sway palm（Fig.3 – 198 ~ 3 – 199）.

3.25.2　**上步提拳**(见图 3 – 200 ~ 3 – 201)。Step foward and raise fist（Fig.3 – 200 ~ 3 – 201）.

图 3 – 198   Fig.3 – 198   图 3 – 199   Fig.3 – 199

图 3 – 200   Fig.3 – 200   图 3 – 201   Fig.3 – 201

3.25.3　弓步栽捶（见图 3 – 202）。Bow stance and punch down（Fig.3 – 202）.

图 3 – 202   Fig. 3 – 202

3.26 斜飞势
Xie Fei Shi（Flying obliquely）

3.26.1 **转身分掌**(见图 3 – 203)。Turn body and open palms（Fig. 3 – 203）.

3.26.2 **上步合掌**(见图 3 – 204)。Step foward and close palms（Fig. 3 – 204）.

3.26.3 **屈膝转身**(见图 3 – 205)。Bend knee and turn body（Fig. 3 – 205）.

图 3 – 203   Fig.3 – 203

图 3 – 204   Fig.3 – 204

图 3 – 205   Fig.3 – 205

图 3 – 206   Fig.3 – 206

3.26.4 弓步斜分（见图 3 – 206）。Bow stance and open palm obliquely（Fig.3 – 206）.

要点：右臂由肩而肘而手节节贯穿列出

Key points：Separate your right arm by moving the shoulder, elbow and hand in turn.

3.27 单鞭下势
Dan Bian Xia Shi（Single whip and push down）

3.27.1 **勾手摆掌**(见图 3 – 207)。Hook hand and sway palm. (Fig.3 – 207).

图 3 – 207　Fig.3 – 207　　　　　图 3 – 208　Fig.3 – 208

3.27.2 **仆步穿掌**(见图 3 – 208)。Crouch stance and pierce palm (Fig.3 – 208).

要点：摆左脚尖、沉胯，身体下沉，保持中正，用腰将右臂节节带回，在通过节节催动穿出。

Key points: Turn left foot outward and lower your body with hips sunk and body upright and centered. The right arm is brought back by the waist and pushed out .

3.28 金鸡独立

Jin Ji Du Li

（Golden rooster stands on one leg）

3.28.1 **弓步起身**(见图3－209)。Bow stance and raise body (Fig.3－209).

要点：起身时，右腿渐渐屈，左腿渐蹬，松腰胯，上体平行前移，劲起于脚传于腰，右膝前领。

Key points: While rising, bend the right leg and push up with the left leg. Relax your waist and hips, and move the upper body forward horizontally. The force comes from the foot to the waist with the right knee bended.

3.28.2 **独立挑掌(左)**(见图3－210)。Stand on one leg and snap palm (left) (Fig.3－210).

要点：右腿支撑身体，膝关节微屈，抽住胯根，用腰劲带动左膝左掌顶挑。

Key points: Bend the right knee which supports your weight and draw back the hips. Use the waist to steer the movements of the left leg and palm.

3.28.3 独立挑掌(右)(见图 3 – 211 ~ 3 – 212)。Stand on one leg and snap palm (right) (Fig. 3 – 211 ~ 3 – 212).

图 3 – 209   Fig. 3 – 209

图 3 – 210   Fig. 3 – 210

图 3 – 211   Fig. 3 – 211

图 3 – 212   Fig. 3 – 212

要点：通过腰的转化，使左掌左脚下落与右掌右脚顶挑，一上一下协调运动。你看过小鸡独立吗？秘密是它的大腿根是放松的，腿中部微屈，脚趾抓地。

Key points: Drop the left palm and foot and thrust up the right palm and foot with coordination. Have you ever seen a rooster standing on one leg? The secret is that it relaxes its thigh and bends its knees with toes gripping the ground.

3.29 退步穿掌
Tui Bu Chuan Zhang
（Step back and pierce palm）

弓步穿掌（见图 3 - 213 ~ 3 - 214）。Bow stance and pierce palms（Fig. 3 - 213 ~ 3 - 214）.

图 3 - 213　Fig. 3 - 213　　　图 3 - 214　Fig. 3 - 214

要点:松左膝,降重心,撤右腿。

Key points:Relax the left hip and lower the weight. Retreat the right leg.

第四段 Segment 4

3.30 虚步压掌
Xu Bu Ya Zhang
（Press palm in empty stance）

3.30.1 扣脚转身(见图 3 – 215 ~ 3 – 216)。Turn foot inward and turn body（Fig. 3 – 215 ~ 3 – 216）.

要点:右脚内扣 90 度。

图 3 – 215   Fig. 3 – 215   图 3 – 216   Fig. 3 – 216

Key points: Turn your right foot 90 degrees inward.

3.30.2 **虚步按掌**(见图 3 - 217 ~ 3 - 218)。Empty stance and Press palm (Fig. 3 - 217 ~ 3 - 218).

图 3 - 217　Fig. 3 - 217　　　　　图 3 - 218　Fig. 3 - 218

3.31　独立托掌
Du Li Tuo Zhang
（**Stand on one leg and raise palm**）

提膝托掌(见图 3 - 219)。Lift knee and raise palm (Fig. 3 - 219).

要点:右掌前撑,左掌外撑,保持平衡状态。

Key points: Push the right palm forward and the left palm aside with balance.

图 3 – 219   Fig. 3 – 219

3.32 马步靠
Ma Bu Kao (Lean and horse stance)

3.32.1 落脚摆掌(见图 3 – 220 ~ 3 – 221)。Drop foot and sway palm (Fig. 3 – 220 ~ 3 – 221),

3.32.2 上步举掌(见图 3 – 222)。Step foward and raise palm (Fig. 3 – 222).

图 3 - 220　Fig.3 - 220　　　　图 3 - 221　Fig.3 - 221

图 3 - 222　Fig.3 - 222

3.32.3　马步靠臂(见图 3 - 223)。Horse stance and lean arm (Fig.3 - 223).

要点：用身体整劲发暗劲。

Key points：Use the force collected from the whole body to lean.

图 3 - 223　Fig. 3 - 223

3.33　转身大捋
Zhuan Shen Da Lu（Turn body and deflect）

3.33.1　摆脚摆掌（见图 3 - 224 ~ 3 - 225）。Turn foot outward and sway palms（Fig. 3 - 224 ~ 3 - 225）.

3.33.2　上步托掌（见图 3 - 226）。Step forward and raise palms（Fig. 3 - 226）.

图 3 – 224　Fig.3 – 224　　　　图 3 – 225　Fig.3 – 225

图 3 – 226　Fig.3 – 226

3.33.3　**转身平捋**（见图 3 – 227 ~ 3 – 228）。Turn body and de-flect horizontally（Fig.3 – 227 ~ 3 – 228）.

图 3 – 227   Fig. 3 – 227

图 3 – 228   Fig. 3 – 228

3.33.4　弓步滚肘(见图 3 – 229)。Bow stance and deflect el -
bow（Fig. 3 – 229）.

　　要点：转身时,碾右脚,滚
臂下压。

Key points：Turn your right
foot and roll your right arm pressing downward while turning your
body.

图 3 – 229   Fig. 3 – 229

3.34 歇步擒打
Xie Bu Qin Da
（Cross legged sitting stance and lock strike）

3.34.1 **拧臂穿拳（见图** 3 – 230 ~ 3 – 231**）。** Twist arm and pierce fist（Fig.3 – 230 ~ 3 – 231）.

图 3 – 230　Fig.3 – 230　　　　　图 3 – 231　Fig.3 – 231

3.34.2 **转体挑掌（见图** 3 – 232**）。** Turn body and snap palm （Fig.3 – 232）.

3.34.3 歇步打拳(见图 3 – 233 ~ 3 – 234)。Cross legged sitting stance and strike fists (Fig. 3 – 233 ~ 3 – 234).

图 3 – 232   Fig. 3 – 232

图 3 – 233   Fig. 3 – 233

图 3 – 234   Fig. 3 – 234

要点：腰的沉拧带动两臂运动。

Key points：Drop and twist your waist to steer the movement of the arms.

3.35　穿掌下势
Chuan Zhang Xia Shi
（Pierce palm and push down）

3.35.1　**收脚举掌**（见图3－235）。Withdraw foot and raise palm（Fig.3－235）.

图3－235　Fig.3－235　　　　图3－236　Fig.3－236

3.35.2　**上步摆掌**（见图3－236）。Step forward and sway palm （Fig.3－236）.

3.35.3 仆步穿掌(见图 3 – 237)。Crouch stance and pierce palms (Fig. 3 – 237).

图 3 – 237　Fig. 3 – 237　　　　图 3 – 238　Fig. 3 – 238

3.36　上步七星
Shang Bu Qi Xing
（Step forward with seven stars）

3.36.1 弓步挑掌(见图 3 – 238)。Bow stance and snap palm (Fig. 3 – 238).

3.36.2 虚步交拳(见图 3 – 239)。Empty stance and cross fists (Fig. 3 – 239).

要点:上右脚时,手脚同时到位,即"手脚相顾",两腕相交背臂撑圆。

图 3 – 239　Fig.3 – 239　　　　图 3 – 240　Fig.3 – 240

Key points：While stepping the right foot forward, complete the movements of hands and feet simultaneously. Cross your wrists and round the back and arms.

3.37　退步跨虎
Tui Bu Kua Hu
（Back step and straddle the tiger）

3.37.1　撤步摆掌（见图 3 – 240）。Retreat step and sway palm (Fig.3 – 240).

3.37.2 **转体落手**(见图 3 – 241)。Turn body and drop hands (Fig.3 – 241).

要点:退步时,重心通过腰胯之间松沉转化,两臂同时对向分开,从上到下劲力一松到脚底。右肘对左膝。

图 3 – 241　Fig.3 – 241　　　　图 3 – 242　Fig.3 – 242

Key points: While stepping back, shift the weight from your waist to hips naturally and separate the arms at the same time. Relax the body from the head to the bottom of feet, and align the right elbow and the left knee.

3.37.3 **独立挑掌**(见图 3 – 242)。Stand on one leg and snap palm(Fig.3 – 242).

3.38 转身摆莲
Zhuan Shen Bai Lian
（Turn body and lotus kick）

3.38.1　落脚摆掌（见图 3 – 243）。Drop foot and sway palm （Fig. 3 – 243）.

图 3 – 243　Fig. 3 – 243

3.38.2　碾脚摆掌（见图 3 – 244）。Pivot foot and sway palm （Fig. 3 – 244）.

要点：分清虚实碾脚。

Key points：Shift the weight with the distinct emptiness and solidness and pivot your foot.

图 3 - 244　Fig. 3 - 244　　　　图 3 - 245　Fig. 3 - 245

3.38.3　**转身翻掌(见图 3 - 345)**。Turn body and palm（Fig. 3 - 245）.

要点;保持以腰脊为转轴,上下一线,转轴与地面垂直。

Key points：Use the backbone as the axis to turn and keep the axis vertical to the floor.

3.38.4　**摆腿拍脚(见图 3 - 246)**。Sway leg and slap foot（Fig. 3 - 246）.

要点：突出以腰为发力之源,手脚互领,上中下协调一致。

Key points：Releasing the force from the waist. Coordinate the movements of the hands and feet .

图 3 – 246　Fig.3 – 246

3.39　弯弓射虎

Wan Gong She Hu（Bend bow to shoot tiger）

3.39.1　屈膝摆掌（见图 3 – 247 ~ 3 – 248）。Bend knee and sway palm（Fig.3 – 247 ~ 3 – 248）.

3.39.2　落步落掌（见图 3 – 249）。Drop foot and palm（Fig.3 – 249）.

3.39.3　转身握拳（见图 3 – 250）。Turn body and clench fist（Fig.3 – 250）.

图 3 – 247　Fig.3 – 247

图 3 – 248　Fig.3 – 248

图 3 – 249　Fig.3 – 249

图 3 – 250　Fig.3 – 250

3.39.4　弓步架冲(见图 3 – 251)。Bow stance and push forward (Fig.3 – 251).

要点：两臂运转，用腰带动，气沉胯松，劲通于背，由下向上贯通，协调用劲。

Key points：Use your waist to steer the movements of the arms. Relax your hips with the "Qi" sunk and make the force flow through the back to the arms.

图 3 – 251　Fig. 3 – 251

3.40　左揽雀尾
Zuo Lan Que Wei
（Left grasp the peacock's tail）

3.40.1　转体落手(见图 3 – 252)。Turn body and drop hands (Fig. 3 – 252).

3.40.2　丁步抱球(见图 3 – 253)。T – stance and hold ball (Fig. 3 – 253).

3.40.3 转体上步(见图 3 – 254)。Turn body and step forward (Fig – 254).

图 3 – 252　Fig.3 – 252

图 3 – 253　Fig.3 – 253

图 3 – 254　Fig.3 – 254

图 3 – 255　Fig.3 – 255

3.40.4 **弓步右掤(见图**3 – 255**)。** Bow stance and right ward off (Fig.3 – 255).

要点:左腿前弓由踝、膝、胯节节依次放松,与左臂协调一致,上下对应贯穿用劲,两臂撑圆。

Key points: Bend the left leg forward in bow stance by relaxing the ankle, the knee and the hips with the coordination of the left arm and push the arms outward with the force.

3.40.5 **转体伸手(见图**3 – 256**)。** Turn body and stretch hands (Fig.3 – 256).

要点:松腰前伸两掌。

Key points: Stretch out arms before relaxing the waist.

图 3 – 256   Fig.3 – 256   图 3 – 257   Fig.3 – 257

3.40.6 **后坐下将**(见图3－257)。Sit back and deflect down-ward (Fig.3－257).

要点:重心后移,右胯根微开后撤,屈膝坐腿,松腰带动两掌侧将。

Key points: Shift your weight back with the right hip slightly opened and retreated backward. Bend your knee and sit back on your leg. Relax the waist to steer the movement of deflecting the palms.

3.40.7 **转体搭手**(见图3－258)。Turn body and place hand against wrist (Fig.2－258).

图3－258　Fig.3－258　　　图3－259　Fig.3－259

3.40.8 **弓步前挤**(见图3－259)。Bow stance and squeeze forward (Fig.3－259).

要点：松左侧腰胯，身体调正，右脚蹬地，左腿前弓，松腰沉胯，挤手协调一致，劲贯左臂尺骨侧。

Key points：Relax your left waist and hip. Adjust the body and keep it centered. Push the right foot against the floor and bend the left leg with the waist relaxed and the hips dropped. Squeeze your hands with the force focused on the left ulna.

3.40.9 翻掌前伸(见图3－260)。Turn palm and stretch forward (Fig.3－260).

图3－260 Fig.3－260   图3－261 Fig.3－261

3.40.10 后坐收掌(见图3－261)。Sit back and draw palm back (Fig.3－261).

要点：松身坐腿带动两臂屈肘回收。
Key points：Relax your body and sit back on your hips to draw

the arms back by bending the elbows.

3.40.11　弓步推按(见图 3 - 262)。Bow stance and push forward (Fig. 3 - 262).

图 3 - 262　Fig. 3 - 262

3.41　十字手
Shi Zi Shou (Cross hands)

3.41.1　扣脚转体(见图 3 - 263)。Turn foot inward and turn body (Fig. 3 - 263).

要点:扣左脚转身,以腰带动两臂平摆。
Key points: Turn your left foot inward and turn your body.

Use the waist to steer the arms swaying across horizontally.

3.41.2 **转身展掌(见图3-264)。** Turn body and widen palms (Fig.3-264).

要点：松右胯，长腰，转身展臂。

Key points：Relax the right hip with your waist stretched. Turn the body and stretch the arms.

图3-263 Fig.3-263   图3-264 Fig.3-264

3.41.3 **收脚合手(见图3-265~3-266)。** Withdraw foot and close hands (Fig.3-265~3-266).

要点：沉左胯，稳住重心，松右胯，收右脚，收右手，重心再移于两脚之间。

Key points：Drop the left hip and keep your weight steady. Relax the right hip to draw in the right hand and foot and shift your weight to the center of both feet.

图 3 – 265　Fig.3 – 265

图 3 – 266　Fig.3 – 266

3.42　收势
Shou Shi（Closing form）

3.42.1　**翻掌分臂**(见图 3 – 267)。Turn palm and open arms (Fig.3 – 267).

3.42.2　**两掌下按**(见图 3 – 268)。Press both palms down (Fig. 3 – 268).

3.42.3 并脚合步(见图 3 – 269 ~ 3 – 270)。Stand with feet together (Fig. 3 – 269 ~ 3 – 270).

图 3 – 267   Fig. 3 – 267

图 3 – 268   Fig. 3 – 268

图 3 – 269   Fig. 3 – 269

图 3 – 270   Fig. 3 – 270

要点：平心静气。

Key points：Calm down with concentration.

附录 1　整个套路动作路线图

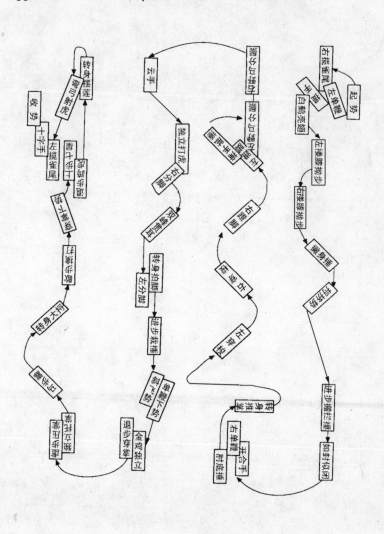

附录 2　　学练太极拳竞赛套路指南

太极拳竞赛套路只是用来竞赛的吗

太极拳竞赛套路虽然名为"竞赛"套路,其实,它的功能绝对不仅仅限于竞赛,它具有明显的健身效果,这是因为竞赛套路具有如下特性:

1.科学性

太极拳竞赛套路注重运用人体运动规律,符合人体生理特点,能促进身心健康,比如竞赛套路的编排一般是由易到难,运动量由小到大,逐渐趋于平缓。

2.全面性

太极拳竞赛套路非常注意左右肢的均衡发展,动作对称分布,而且技术内容丰富,非常利于人体全面锻炼,促进身心健康。

3.适应性

各式太极拳竞赛套路,能满足不同人的需求,为了健身的需要,竞赛套路完全可以根据具体情况而变化,具有良好的适应性,比如老年人学练时,完全可以不做难度大的动作,去掉或降低一定的动作数量及要求,还可因自身条件而决定做哪些动作。据北京体育大学对各式太极拳竞赛套路的科学研究证实,长期坚持学练太极拳竞赛套路,能够恢复和增强神经、血液循环、消化等各大系统的功能,具有良好的健身作用。

如何选练太极拳竞赛套路

1.因人因式

每个人的身体情况、性格爱好、生理特点不同,选练太极拳竞赛套路时首先应该考虑到自身的这些条件,然后,根据各式太极拳竞赛套路的特点,选择适合自己的一式入手学练。比如身体健壮、喜欢发力的中青年人,选择陈式太极拳竞赛套路为好;年龄偏大、体质较弱的人,选择步高架活的孙式太极拳竞赛套路为宜;性格温和、喜欢安静的人,选择杨式太极拳竞赛套路较适合。总之,选择适合自己的套路学练,往往能事半功倍,收到良好的健身、竞赛效果。

2.因势因果

为了竞赛而学练太极拳竞赛套路时,除了考虑自身特点外,还应根据各式太极拳竞赛的形势和预期结果而选项,比如全国、国际的太极拳竞赛中,男女 42 式太极拳、太极剑参赛人数多、水平高,男子陈式太极拳水平较高,女子杨式太极拳竞争较激烈,而男子孙式太极拳、女子陈式太极拳以及男女武式太极拳、吴式太极拳参赛人数较少,竞争相对弱些,对于一般选手而言,应选取相对容易取得名次的项目作为突破口。

如何学好太极拳竞赛套路

1.满怀信心,明确目标

学好太极拳竞赛套路,首先应该满怀信心,明确目标。如果是为了健身,就一定要坚信,学练太极拳能促进身心健康。如果是为了竞赛,就要有必胜的信心,不怕困难与挫折,不断进取,不懈努力,相信功夫不负有心人。

2.读书看盘,投师访友

随着信息技术的飞速发展,学练者可以通过文字、声像及多媒体的教材,认真读书钻研,观摩示范,是学好太极拳竞赛套路的重要手段之一,甚至能无师自通。实践证明,有相当一部分人是通过这种渠道的学练,不仅练好了身体,而且,还在竞赛中取得了好成绩。当然,在自己看光盘、读书学习的基础上,有条件的尽可能请名师指导,口传身授,会有意想不到的收获。

3.循序渐进,精益求精

初学太极拳竞赛套路,应该循序渐进,不可贪多求快。应本着精益求精的思想,反复学习每一个动作,包括定型动作、要点、方位轨迹等都要清清楚楚,以免养成错误的动作习惯,影响整个技术的提高,以及健身竞赛效果。自学的方法最好是动静结合,所谓动是要跟着光盘学练,动起来;所谓静是要认真看书中的图解,仔细琢磨,一个动作一个动作的推敲学习,切记不要囫囵吞枣,贪多求快。

如何练好太极拳竞赛套路

1.打好基础,勤练不辍

基础练习包括太极拳的基本身心素质、基本动作等内容,要练好太极拳竞赛套路,这是基石,否则难以构筑技术高峰。必须打好扎实的基础,对必要的柔韧素质、平衡能力、基本动作要进行严格、艰苦和勤奋练习,即使达到了一定水平,也不能放松,绝不能丢弃基础性练习,这是成功的保证。如本系列丛书提供的各式太极拳和太极剑的静桩、动桩,就是十分有效的基础练习内容,需要贯彻始终,勤练不辍。

2.抓住核心,意形兼练

太极拳竞赛套路都有明确的技术要求,本系列丛书介绍了各式太极拳的核心技术,抓住这些技术进行学练,会事半功倍地提高你的水平。在看书的同时,还要注意观看光盘的示范,体会太极拳的意气神韵,突出太极拳运动的特点,这也是练好太极拳竞赛套路的关键,防止练拳时不讲意识引导动作,失去劲力内涵,演化成太极操。

如何参加太极拳竞赛套路的竞赛

1.遵守规则,注意细节

由于太极拳竞赛套路有明确统一的动作规则,竞赛中裁判员一般都依据规则来评判,所以要尽可能按照规则要求做动作,避免所做动作与套路规则内容不符,出现动作方向、数量与规则不同的错误,以至造成不必要的扣分。这里需要特别注意,有时看书学套路不容易学到位,比如,陈式太极拳竞赛套路早期的版本中,起势动作中有划圈的描写,但是,幅度不大,而我们在实际的教学中划的是大圈,这些细节应仔细看光盘学习。还有一点要特别注意,就是每次竞赛时规程的要求以及大会对动作规则的补充通知,比如同样的套路动作,由于裁判长以及裁判员对动作规则理解的差异,或者是由于对套路个别地方的修改,会造成每次竞赛有细微的差别,这也会造成不必要的扣分。如 42 式太极剑在脚跟、脚尖落地,摆扣等问题上就有所差异,这些在竞赛前最好能取得裁判的统一认识。

2.提高素质,避免紧张

竞赛时几乎每个人或多或少都有些紧张,赛场上常常可以看到运动员手脚发抖、失去平衡、动作变形的现象,这些很大程度是由心理因素造成的。据统计,遥测全国太极拳竞赛场上运动员心率,有的高达 180 次/分。本不属于大强度运动的太极拳,为什么有如此高的心率反应呢? 主要还是紧张造成的,按太极拳的技术要求应该是"心静体松"。但是,由于竞赛很难让运动员心理真正放松,所以,首先要让运动员正确认识和对待紧张。紧张是一种正常的生理、心理现象,几乎是每个人都有,只是程度不同而已,不必恐惧焦虑。其次,有意增加模拟性竞赛练习,提高心理素质。第三,出现极度紧张,往往是在分脚独立时产生,所以要加强相关动作所需身体素质的练习。最后,不妨从学练太极拳竞赛套路中找原因,看看自己是否按太极拳运动要领学练的,虚领顶劲,以意导体,气沉丹田,排除杂念。总之,逐渐通过综合性学练提高心理素质、身体素质、技术水平,减小紧张程度。

3.做好准备,适时上场

竞赛前合理有效的准备活动能明显提高竞赛成绩。这里应包括对场地地质、演练方向、准备活动时间等方面的了解。一般来讲,距上场前20~30分钟做准备活动较好,轻微慢跑、比划套路、重点动作练习等均为主要准备活动内容,以身体微微出汗、周身舒服为度,脉搏控制在120次/分以下较为适宜。当然,每个人的习惯不同,不必强求,以能活动开、发挥最好技术水平为准。另外,还要注意到赛场的场地情况,有无地毯、地毯的质地如何、上场时是几个人、站位情况、演练的方向要求、所穿鞋的厚薄质地等,这些小问题,也必须重视,否则会因小失大。

各式太极拳竞赛套路的风格特点是什么,学练中怎样注意相关的技术差异

各式太极拳竞赛套路有着很多共性的地方,比如都要求用意识引导动作,刚柔相济,相对缓慢等;动作名称、套路结构相似等。但是,各式太极拳竞赛套路又有着各自不同的特点,具体的技术差异表现为:

1.陈式太极拳竞赛套路

陈式太极拳竞赛套路节奏鲜明,气势宏大。练习中,要突出缠丝劲法及松活弹抖的发力,表现出陈式太极拳竞赛套路独特的风格特点。具体表现在以躯干的缠绕为主,通过腰脊的螺旋转动和胸腹的折叠变化来贯串上肢和下肢的螺旋缠丝,达到周身缠丝。外形上,上肢两臂旋腕转膀,形如拧麻花状;下肢两腿旋踝转腿,似拧钻螺丝之形。发力上,防止过分追求发力效果,以至于发僵直劲,或发虚假劲。发力后尤其注意与下边动作的自然衔接,避免断劲。

解决方法:要发好力,应由"极柔软"再至"极坚刚"。开始时多注意由内动引导肢体的放长,螺旋缠绕,逐渐发力,还应专门进行单势发力练习及其他辅助练习如柔韧性练习,抖大杆子等。

陈式太极拳竞赛套路手型也很特殊,不同于其他式太极拳竞赛套路的手型,主要表现为掌型为瓦楞形的螺旋状,大拇指根合向小指,指尖后仰,这与陈式特点及技击作用有关,练习时应注意,防止陈式、杨式掌型混同。陈式的勾型是五指尖自然捏拢也不同于其他式,应引起大家注意。擦脚出步是陈式的步法特点。往往有擦不着脚的问题,除了与地质有关外,主要是与虚实、腿力大小有关。另外,还应正确掌握擦脚的距离。平时要专门练习步法,加强腿力练习(以桩功为主)。

2.杨式太极拳竞赛套路

杨式太极拳竞赛套路重点突出动作外形的舒展大方,动作过程的柔和缓慢。整个套路具有连贯圆活、沉稳舒展、形象优美的独特风格。防止过分追求动作柔、姿势低、幅度大、造型美,造成动作变形,出现跪膝、拔跟毛病;动作轻飘,出现柔软操化、失去轻灵中的沉稳,没有内劲。

解决方法:在规定动作基础上,强调太极拳技术要求,适当的辅以功法、推手练习,来帮助学练者正确理解太极拳运动本质特点,保持项目自身的特色。

3.武式太极拳竞赛套路

武式太极拳竞赛套路有自己突出的特色,每个动作的过程都有"起、承、开、合"的要求。从动作外形看,在一个个节序之间似有稍顿的现象,但是,实际上动作意识并没有断,只是在贯劲,追求内动、内劲,而且每个动作都有这4个过程,有时是几个完整拳势被列入一个节序,但同样要有起承开合过程,这是一个重要特色。

防止练习时每个动作节序不清,动作不到位,一滑而过,失去武式风格。练习时,首先要从动作外形上,区别开4个过程,可以分开练,然后逐渐再连贯。

两手不出足尖也是武式太极拳竞赛套路独特的特点之一。武式太极拳竞赛套路有严格的要求,要求出手对应前脚尖,不能超出,所谓手不出足尖。很多习惯了其他式太极拳竞赛套路的人开始不容易做到这一要求。

解决方法:首先在思想认识上,明确武式太极拳竞赛套路的特点,然后再从技术上找方法,其主要方法是从关节角度上找及通过体表的标志训练慢慢养成习惯。

左右手不相逾越的要求,也是其他式太极拳竞赛套路爱好者和初学者不容易做到的技术,关键在腰的带动上,这应从身法上去练习,适当时可以用标志物限定手的轨迹。如用衣服的拉链位置,胸部的心口窝处等做参照物,限定两手的运动轨迹。

武式太极拳竞赛套路的身法特点也十分突出,要点有:含胸、拔背、裹裆、护腕、提顶、吊裆、松肩、沉肘、腾挪、闪战、尾闾正中、气沉丹田、虚实分清,这些在具体动作中,要认真体会。

4.吴式太极拳竞赛套路

吴式太极拳竞赛套路具有鲜明的技术特色,主要表现在身型上,"斜中寓正",即讲究弓腿、重心偏向前腿,如搂膝拗步、倒卷肱、上步揽雀尾、斜飞势等,看上去上体稍向前倾,而实际上头前脚后,从头顶(百会)到后脚跟,中间通过裆部,形成三点连成一条斜向地面的直线,即所谓"斜中寓正"。

步型上,突出"川"字步型,即两脚掌近似平行,脚尖、脚跟都向前;弓步步型要求前弓腿的膝与脚尖上下相对,弓步的两脚如同踏在"川"字两端上;虚步步型,要求也像"川"字一样,即虚脚点在"川"字的中竖上。还有一个特点是吴式太极拳竞赛套路中有马步,也叫桩步,其他各式太极拳竞赛套路没有明显定势的马步。手型上强调虎口张圆,拇指上竖。

学练中,注意防止为了追求"斜中寓正"而斜中不正,出现俯身、折腰、撅臀的毛病;弓步时前膝超出脚尖、后脚跟拔起、两脚之间不平行等毛病。

解决方法:首先正确理解吴式太极拳竞赛套路的风格特点,然后,增加典型动作的单势练习,适当时候可以采用客观标志物限定的方法练习。如吴式太极拳的进步练习,可以在地上做两条与肩同宽的标志线,两脚踩在线上练习,同时,辅以踝关节的柔韧练习,如压踝、揉踝等。

5.孙式太极拳竞赛套路

孙式太极拳竞赛套路的步法讲究进退相随,进步必跟、退步必撤,这是其主要技术特征之一,要求"迈步如槐虫蠕动,往来似水漂落叶",体现出步活、步点准确、步幅适中、步态轻灵的特色。迈步时,两脚始终在虚实转换当中平稳过渡,常常在裆下沉中,重心转换,而且要求身体平稳移动,没有明显的起伏。后脚跟步时,与前脚相距10厘米左右,要暗含蹬劲。退步时,松腰、沉胯反向回收脚,一进一退像是在一个浅弧形上滑动,沉稳匀速。

练习时,常出现跟步时被动提后脚,重心平移,没有内劲变化以及跟步的步点不准,距离前脚跟太近或过远,扣脚时踩脚,步态轻浮没有沉劲等毛病。

解决方法:首先,认识到步法特点的实质,然后,采用标志物(如划线)限定步幅、步点等方法,专门练习进退步法。

手法上的开合又是孙式太极拳竞赛套路的另一个重要特点。做开合手时要注意胸部气息的变化,保持坠肘、沉肩的状态。防止张肘式的开合,没有气感内劲。

解决方法:可以用阻力、助力的外力刺激,正确体会动作要点,如两掌心顶一根与脸同宽的尺子或木棍,站开手桩,解决开手两掌外翻掌心不相对的毛病。

6.42式太极拳竞赛套路

42式太极拳竞赛套路是以竞赛为主要目的、突出了规范性,包括动作外形、方位、路线等,在学练中这方面要按规则严格细抠。由于竞赛套路中兼有各式太极拳动作,往往令人不知如何做这些动作,其实,按规则及编创主旨,42式太极拳竞赛套路的风格特点与以往48式太极拳相同,基本上以杨式太极拳风格为主,对于其他式的动作这里也按"杨式"处理,但是仍要保留原动作的基本造型及基本特点,如"掩手肱捶"还要发力,但与陈式中的发力在动作的手型、步型上有所变化。再如"玉女穿梭"虽然吸收吴式的平云手法,但是身型上以中正为主,不做吴式的"斜中寓正'等等,这些应该引起注意。

7.42式太极剑竞赛套路

42式太极剑竞赛套路是目前与42式太极拳配套的惟一的一项太极拳器械竞赛套路,有的竞赛将拳和剑的成绩累加取全能名次。42式太极剑竞赛套路,主要吸收了传统杨式、吴式、陈式等太极剑的内容,以杨式太极剑的动作为主,整个套路的风格特点与42式太极拳一致,主要技术风格特点为:剑正势美、气贯剑器、轻灵沉稳、剑势缠绵、柔中寓刚、刚发剑响。

练习中最大的问题是,身与剑不合一,剑法不清楚。

解决方法:①先拳后剑,打好基础。练好太极拳是学练太极剑的基础。在太极剑中用到的身型、身法、步型、步法以及眼法,都与太极拳一致,通过徒手拳术练习,掌握虚领顶劲、含胸拔背、连贯圆活、弧形运动等有关太极拳要求,进而练习太极剑术。②循序渐进,力求准确。初学太极剑,一招一势要力求准确。手、步、身、眼和剑法都要概念清楚,符合规范,切不可贪多求速,不求甚解,以免形成错误定型,造成"学拳容易改拳难"的局面。③先形后意,形意统一。太极剑是以意气主导的剑术,但在刚开始练剑时,还应该先重视动作外形(主要是剑法的规格),比如劈剑与点剑的区别、撩剑的运行路线等。正确的外形是用意的必备条件,当然形与意不可分,正确的用意又能促进正确外形的形成,这只是剑术练习的不同阶段侧重点不同而已,最终还是要用意导剑,形意统一,进而达到"神明"境界,动作高度自动化,形、意、神、剑合一。

Appendix 2

A Guide to Learning and Practicing the Competition Routines of Tai Ji Quan

Is the Competition Routine Only Used for Competition

Although the competition routine of Tai Ji Quan is branded as the "competition style", its function is not restricted to the competition only. It has the obvious affections on keeping fit because of the following characteristics the competition style has.

1. Scientifically designed

The competition routine emphasizes the biomechanical principles that are in accordance to the physiological structure of the body. This helps improve both mental and physical health. For example, the format of the competition routines is arranged in sequence according to its difficulty —— from the easy to the difficult ones, and the strength needed in the routine —— from the weak to the strong.

2. Overall completeness

The competition routine of Tai Ji Quan pays close attention to the balance development between the right and left parts of the body including a symmetrical layout of the movements. Besides, it is rich in its technical contents thus providing a beneficial overall workout for your health.

3. Adaptability

In order to efficiently serve its health purposes, the competition routine is accustomed to change according to the specific situations due to its adaptability. For the aged people, they are not obliged to perform the difficult movements but reducing the amount of movements or lowering the demands. They can also choose to perform certain movements according to their own health conditions. According to the research done by Beijing Sport University in the different styles of Tai Ji Quan, it has been proven that the long term training in the competition routines can recover and improve the nerve system, blood circulation, digestion and other major systems of the body with good affections for health.

How to Choose the Right Competition Routine for Yourself

1. Depends on the learner and the characteristics of different styles

People have different physical conditions, preferences and health, therefore, you should take all these into considerations before choosing one of the styles. After that, pick up the style that is suitable for yourself. For example, for young people who usually have stronger physique and more energy, it is better to choose Chen style. For the elders or those with weaker physique, Sun style will be more suitable as it has less strenuous stances. For those who prefer tranquility, or those with a mild character, they will find Yang style more appealing. In conclusion, choosing the right style of Tai Ji Quan will help you to have a more enjoyable and less stressful training, and to benefit you both in your health and in your competition.

2. Depends on the goal of the individual and the circumstances

For those who choose to learn the competition routine of Tai Ji Quan solely for the purpose of competing in Tai Ji Quan competitions, you should consider the trends of a certain competition style to choose besides his own physical conditions. For example, in the national and the international competitions, there are more participants in 42 style Tai Ji Quan and Tai Ji Jian both in Men's and Women's, so the competitions are fierce. For male, the competition routine of Chen style has a higher standard while for female, it's Yang style. Whereas Men's Sun style, Women's Chen style and Men's and Women's Wu style have less participants and the competition is comparatively weak. For general participants, it is wise to choose those that you may have more chance to win.

How to Learn the Competition Routines of Tai Ji Quan

1. Be confident with definite goals

To have a strong confidence and a focused goal are the most important factors when learning the competition routine of Tai Ji Quan. For those who learn to keep fit, they must have the faith that learning and practicing Tai Ji Quan will bring them the bene-fits. For those who learn for participating in the competitions, they'll have to have the strong will to win. They shouldn't be afraid of the tough training and the unavoidable setbacks, and should try to strive for every possible chance for the improvement.

2. Be well read and well informed

With the development of information technology, the learners could further enhance their knowledge and perfect their skills through reading books, listening to recorders and even using the multimedia resources, such as video tapes and VCDs. Some-times, to the extent, that you can master the competition routines even without a coach in person. Quite a number of people are known to have learned and practiced Tai Ji Quan by using the mul-timedia teaching materials and some even won places in competi-tions besides keeping fit. But of course, if given a chance, it is al-ways more beneficial to learn personally from masters.

3. Learn and practice systematically to perfect your skills

In the early stage of learning and practicing Tai Ji Quan, you should always try to improve your skills systematically. It is not wise to learn too much or hasten the learning pace, instead try to perfect your skills of every single movement by practicing again and again until you fully master it in case you form bad habits which will affect both your improvement of skills and scores in competitions. If you are learning Tai Ji Quan on your own(as op-posed to learning from a master in person), the best way is to combine the "motion" and "motionless" aspects of Tai Ji Quan. This so called motion means to follow the video tape or VCD and practice accordingly. This so called motionless means to read the key points intensively, and pay special attention to the photographs of each movement.

How to Master the Competition Routine of Tai Ji Quan

1. Learn the basics and practice regularly

The basic practice includes the practice of the basic mentality and the movement etc. which are the foundation required to master the competition routine of Tai Ji Quan, otherwise, it will be really difficult to reach a high level. It is necessary to acquire the flexibility, balance and learn the basic movements through the strict, intensive and diligent training. Even after reaching a competent level, you should still need to keep on practicing the basics which can be the best guarantee to your success. For instance, the motionless and moving stances of different styles of Tai Ji Quan and Tai Ji Jian provided by this book are the best basic exercises which you need to practice regularly.

2. Focus on the key points and have a balanced training on both the mind and the movements

All the competition routines of Tai Ji Quan have strict technical requirements and this series provides a clear illustration of the important techniques of all the competition routines of different Tai Ji Quan styles. Mastering these important techniques will bring you a speedy and steady improvement in your skills. Apart from reading, it is also crucial to follow the demonstrations in the VCD which comes together with the books in order to understand the important aspects and features of Tai Ji Quan. It is also a good way to prevent you from performing the movements without any internal forces or meanings.

Important Hints When Taking Part in the Competitions of the Competition Routine of Tai Ji Quan

1. Obey the rules and regulations, and notice the important details

Due to the fact that there are definitive standards of performance regarding the competition routines, the referees usually judge the performance according to these standard rules. Therefore it is important for the participants to perform according to what is required in the standard and avoid the situations which would constitute violations and result in unnecessary point deductions. You should be aware that it is sometimes difficult to get the right posture when learning from books alone. For example, in the earlier version of the competition routine of Chen style, it is required to display a small circular movement at the beginning while in actual practice, what we do is a slightly bigger circular movement. That's the reason why you should refer to the videos on these differences. You should also pay special attention to the notification of changes issued before every competition which usually contains the latest amendments on the rules and the movement requirements. Sometimes the chief judge and the referees might have different interpretations regarding the movement requirements and that will some times result in slight changes in the competition process and the point deductions if you are unaware of them. For example, in the 42 style of Tai Ji Jian, there are some differences in turning foot inward and landing the heel and toes. So you should try your best to get a mutual understanding with the referees about the requirements before the competition.

2. **Improve your mentality and avoid getting too nervous during the competition**

Almost everybody gets nervous during the competition with the symptoms of the shaky limbs, losing balance or making wrong movements which are mainly caused by mental factors. Some participants may have their hearts beat as fast as 180 times per minute. Why do they have such a high heart rate while performing this less strength demanded sports? According to the studies, this is mainly due to the nervousness. We know that the technical requirement for Tai Ji Quan is "to have a peaceful mind and a relaxed body" but the competitions will definitely affect the state of your mind. Therefore the important thing is to let yourself learn to control yourself. Firstly, you need to understand that it is natural to feel nervous, so there is no need to worry about it. Secondly, you can improve your mental readiness by participating in the simulation practices. Thirdly, the extreme nervousness usually happens when performing the difficult movements like "standing on one leg". Therefore putting more effort and attention in such movements is a good way to overcome such difficulties. Lastly, it would be helpful to learn about your faults during your practice and check whether the movements are performed according to the requirements of Tai Ji Quan. In general, you can reduce your nervousness by improving the quality of your mind, your physique and your skills.

3. Get ready in advance and begin on time

Appropriate and sufficient preparations in advance will be helpful in getting good results during the competition. The preparations include a good knowledge of the competition ground, the direction of the performance and the duration allowed for warming up. In most cases, it is advisable to begin warming up 20 ~ 30 minutes before the competition by jogging slowly, rehearsing the full set of the routine or concentrating on the important movements. Warming up exercise is considered sufficient when you begin to perspire slightly and feel comfortable with the pulse rate around 120 times per minute. This is not, however, a universal standard for every participant since everybody has his own habits and body conditions. It is considered the best when you can best display your skills. The conditions of the competition grounds is also important. You should check whether it is carpeted, and if so, check the quality of the carpet. You should also check how many participants will be allowed to perform simultaneously and the position of yours. The direction of the performance (to the referees and judges accordingly) and the quality of the allowed costumes are also important points you need to notice.

What Are the Special Characteristics in the Competition Routines of the Different Styles of Tai Ji Quan

The competition routines of different styles of Tai Ji Quan share a lot of common characteristics such as "using your mind to guide your movements, combining the softness and the hardness and having the similar structures and names of the movements" etc. But surely each has its own specific characteristics. The details of the differences are as the followings:

1. The competition routine of Chen style Tai Ji Quan

The competition routine of Chen style Tai Ji Quan is famous for its distinctive rhythm and the magnificent postures. When practicing, it is important to emphasize on the "spiral twisting force" and the basic requirements of relaxing, agility and springing which are the special features of Chen style Tai Ji Quan. The movements stress on the twisting of the torso. The twisting force of the upper and lower limbs are connected through the twisting motion of the spine and the changes of folding in the chest and the abdomen in order to obtain a full twisting force all over the body. For the upper limbs, twist the arm and wrist in coordinately like twisting a wet cloth dry. For the lower limbs, twist the ankles, the thighs and the calves in like driving in a screw. For the force, you should avoid over emphasize releasing the force which would result in displaying a stiff force or a false one. After releasing the force, it is imperative to maintain the continuity with the next movements without the severance in the force.

Methods to overcome such obstacles: In order to master the correct techniques of the force releasing, you should bear in mind that it is "from the extreme softness to the extreme hardness". At the beginning, you should emphasize the extension of the body movements from the internal motions to the twisting motions and finally to the external releasing of the force. It is also important to specifically train the force releasing of individual movement and other supplementary exercises such as the exercises of the flexibility and the "pole trembling" exercise.

The hand forms of Chen style Tai Ji Quan are also different from other Tai Ji Quan techniques. The main difference is that the palm is in the form of a Chinese tile and slightly retracted inward with the thumb and the little finger slightly folded and facing each other, and the tip of finger slightly pointed backward. This is in agreement with its attacking features and a distinctive difference of Chen style from others, so you should remember not to confuse it with other styles of Tai Ji Quan. The "hook form" of Chen style is also different as it is a natural clutching of all fingers. For the footwork, rubbing the moving foot with the stationary one before treading out is also a distinctive feature of Chen style. Sometimes the learners missed the rubbing motion, it is usually related to the strength in the footwork and the understanding of the "emptiness and solidity" besides the differences in the ground quality. In addition, accuracy regarding where and when the feet should rub against each other is also of great importance. You should specifically train the footwork techniques separately, and should strengthen the legs and feet through practicing standing stances.

2. The competition routine of Yang style Tai Ji Quan

The competition routine of Yang style emphasize the out – stretched and open – handed movements which are more gentle and slightly slower than others. The whole set has the features of the coherence, agility, outstretching with steadiness and elegance. You should avoid over emphasize the gentleness and the low posture or over extend the movements and paying too much attention to the visual attractiveness which would easily result in the distortion of the movements like kneeling posture and lifting heels. Over emphasize the gentleness will also result in transforming this routine into a calisthenics drill and failing to display its stability and strength.

Methods to overcome such obstacles: Focus on the key techniques of Tai Ji Quan besides practicing the standard movements. You should supplement your daily practice with the training methods such as the hand pushing exercise to understand the key and basics of Tai Ji Quan and maintain the special features of this style.

3. The competition routine of Wu style(武式) Tai Ji Quan

The Wu style has very prominent characteristics. Every movement strictly follows the sequence of the"commence, succession, open and close". By looking at its movement you can easily discover that although there is a consistent intermission between every major connection of movements, the momentum is not in anyway broken but carried through with the special emphasis on the internal movements and the internal strength. Sometimes a few complete movements are grouped into one combination but it still follows the sequence. This is the distinctive characteristic of Wu style.

It is important for you to avoid the ambiguous and incorrect display of the movements and the omission of the necessary sequences in case losing the color of Wu style Tai Ji Quan. When practicing, it is advisable to practice them separately by breaking the external movements into 4 sequences before connecting them up.

Another one of the characteristics of Wu style is never let

your hands extend over your feet. Wu styly has the strict requirement that the hands should be corresponded with the feet by not extending over the toes. Many practitioners who are used to practicing other competition routines are not used to this requirement.

Methods to overcome such obstacles: Understand the characteristics of Wu style Tai Ji Quan first and try to find out the ways in technique. The main method is to practice the angle of the joints, portray it onto the body postures through training and gradually form into a habit.

It is also a difficult skill for the beginners and many practitioners of other Tai Ji Quan styles in not being allowed to overlap the left and right hands. The key is the movement of the waist. You can start from training your body movements such as using signs to guide the trail of the hands. The signs can be the zip of the coat or your chest where you can refer to limit the trail of your hands.

The characteristics of the body movements in the competition routine of Wu style is very prominent. The key points are as the followings: Keep your chest in, stretch the back, round the crotch, protect the wrist, lift your head, hold the crotch, drop the shoulders and elbows, jump, deflect, align the coccyx, sink the "Qi" down to "Dan Tien", and clarify the emptiness and solidness.

4. The competition routine of Wu style(吴式) Tai Ji Quan

The competition routine of Wu style Tai Ji Quan has the significant characteristics mainly portrayed in its body posture "upright when slanting". It emphasizes the bow stance while having the weight leaning forward such as "brush knee and twist step", "step back and whirl arms", "step forward to grasp the peacock's tail" and "fly obliquely" etc. For the posture, it seems that the body is leaning forward while actually, from the head to the heel through the buttocks, the 3 points form a straight line slanting towards the ground which is known as the "upright when slanting".

In footwork, it focuses on stance of the Chinese character "川". Both feet are paralleled with the tips and the heels facing the same direction. The footwork in bow stance requires the knee of the front leg in alignment with the toes. Both feet in bow stance is alike stepping on the edges of the Chinese character "川". The requirement for the footwork in empty stance is also on the character "川" by having the empty foot placed onto the center line of the character. Another characteristic in Wu style Tai Ji Quan is its "horse stance", in another name known as the "pile stance" which other styles of Tai Ji Quan seldom have. Its hand postures emphasize the opening of the "tiger mouth" with the thumb facing upward.

When practicing, try to avoid the movements of leaning the body, folding in the waist and pushing the buttocks out by seeking the "upright when slanting" posture. Don't extend the knees beyond the toes or lift up the heels without keeping the balance between both feet etc.

Methods to overcome such obstacles: Understand the characteristics of Wu style Tai Ji Quan first and after that, add the practice of the single movements and use the guiding signs for training when necessary. For example, the training in footwork of Wu style Tai Ji Quan can be done by drawing 2 parallel lines according to the width of the shoulder and place the feet onto each of the lines. Do the supplementary exercises such as stretching the ankles for accompanying.

5. The competition routine of Sun style Tai Ji Quan

The footwork of the combined advancing and retreating is one of the main characteristics of Sun style Tai Ji Quan. It requires the "follow up step" when advancing and the "draw in step" when retreating just like a worm wriggling and the leaf floating in the water. The routine presents the liveliness when moving, precision in its paces, suitable distance in its steps, lightness and agility in its footwork. When stepping up, move your legs steadily between the emptiness and the solidness with your weight sunk in the center under the crotch. While shifting the weight, keep the body steady without the obvious ups and downs. When the hind leg follows up onto the fore leg, the distance in between is approximately 10 cm and a springing force should also be concealed within the movement. When retreating, relax the waist, sink the crotch down and draw in your leg. The advancing and retreating should be performed like sliding on an arc in the steady and even speed.

During practice, such faults often occur: the hind leg is forced to lift up when stepping forward; when shifting the weight, there's no changes in the internal strength and the landing point is not precise; the distance between both feet is either too close or too far; you may step onto the other foot when turning foot inward and the steps may be drifted without a sunken strength.

Methods to overcome such obstacles:

First, understand the essential character of the footwork. Then, practice the advancing and retreating with the aid of the signs and marks (such as drawing lines on the ground) to limit the distance and the landing points of the steps.

The opening and closing of hands is another important characteristic in the competition routine of Sun style. When opening or closing hands, pay attention to the changes of your chest during the breath with the elbows and the shoulders sunk and prevent the elbows from lifting up or lacking of the internal force and the "Qi".

Methods to overcome such obstacles: Properly understand the essentials of the movement by using the stimulation of the external force, such as the resistant force and the supporting force and the key points of the movement. You can hold a ruler or a stick with the same length as your face and form the opening hands stance to overcome the wrong movements of the hands.

6. The competition routine of 42 style Tai Ji Quan

The competition routine of 42 style is mainly designed for the purpose of competing. It is being standardized in its movements, the positions and the layout. When practicing, you should follow the strict rules and refine every movement. As there are many styles used in this routine, people often get confused on how they should perform these movements. In fact, according to the regulations and the arrangements of the routine, the characteristics of this routine are very similar to that of 48 style Tai Ji Quan which are mainly adopted from Yang style. The movements of other styles are also carried out in the manner of Yang style but remained the original posture of the movements. For example, the movement of "cover and strike fist" taken from Chen style still requires the releasing force but modified in the footwork and hand postures. Another example is the "Jade girl working with shuttles" taken from Wu(吴) style, the body is kept upright instead of keeping it "upright when slanting".

7. The competition routine of 42 style Tai Ji Jian

At present, the competition routine of 42 style Tai Ji Jian is the only weaponry competition style to go along with the competition routine of 42 style Tai Ji Quan. In some competitions the scores for both 42 style Tai Ji Quan and Tai Ji Jian are accumulated and the winner will be given an all – round award. This competition routine of Tai Ji Jian was designed based on the traditional movements of Yang, Wu(吴), and Chen style Tai Ji Jian with more emphasis on Yang style. This competition style shares the similar traits with the competition routine of 42 style Tai Ji Quan and the technical characteristics are as the followings: The posture is elegant with the force penetrated onto the sword and the movements are agile and steady with the well balanced softness and hardness.

The most common difficulty the learners face when practicing this routine is the coordination of the body movements and the ambiguity of the sword movements.

Methods to overcome the obstacles: a) Master the movements of Tai Ji Quan before learning the movements of Tai Ji Jian. You have to master the basics before advancing to the higher levels. Tai Ji Quan is the basis for Tai Ji Jian because the body movements, stances and footwork used in Tai Ji Jian are identical to Tai Ji Quan. You can understand the important techniques of Tai Ji Jian by practicing Tai Ji Quan and apply them to the swordplay. b) Learn the routine systematically and focus on the accuracy in movements. For the beginners, it is crucial to perform every movement precisely according to the key points. The beginners should avoid learning too many movements at a time without fully

understanding the important points of each in case to form the for-
mation of the wrong movements and the bad habits which will be
very difficult to correct later. c) Master the movements before
practicing your mind and then combine the movements and your
mind into one. Tai Ji Jian is the swordplay guided by your mind
and the "Qi". However, when you begin to practice the sword,
you should first pay attention to the external movements (mainly
the regulations of the sword) such as the differences between
striking sword and pointing sword and the route of the waving
sword etc. The correct external movement is the precondition in
using your mind whereas, of course, the form and mind are not
completely separated. This is only the different stages of practicing the sword. If the mind is used correctly, it can increase the
accuracy of the movements. What we want to achieve at last is to
use your mind to guide your sword and to combine both the sword
and the mind into one to reaching the high level of unifying the
form, mind, spirit and sword into one.